STALKING THE WILD PENDULUM

Stalking The Wild Pendulum

On the Mechanics of Consciousness

ITZHAK BENTOV

Destiny Books
Rochester, Vermont

Destiny Books
One Park Street
Rochester, Vermont 05767
www.InnerTraditions.com

Destiny Books is a division of Inner Traditions International

First Quality Paperback edition 1988 by Destiny Books
Copyright © 1977 Itzak Bentov
Copyright © 1988 Mirtala Bentov

LIBRARY OF CONGRESS CATALOGING-IN-PUBLICATION DATA

Bentov, Itzak.
    Stalking the wild pendulum : on the mechanics of consciousness by Itzak
Bentov.
        p.   cm.
    Originally published: New York: E.P. Dutton, ©1977.
    Blibliography:p.
    ISBN 978-089281202-8
    1. Consciousness. 02. Cosmology. I. Title
BF311.B453 1988
126—dc19   87-36458

Printed and bound in China by Reliance Printing Co., Ltd.

40 39 38 37 36 35 34 33 32

ACKNOWLEDGEMENTS

During the time that this book was written, I conferred with many people, mostly scientists who are specialists in their respective fields, to check out the details of my ideas. This fact does not imply in any way that all of them agree with the material presented here.

First, I would like to express my gratitude to Professor Mael Melvin, physicist at Temple University, for going over the manuscript and straightening out my physics, which was limping in places; and to Professor William W. Tiller, Materials Sciences Department, Stanford University, for our long discussions about the nature of the universe and for his writing a preface to this book. To Tom Etter, physicist, University of Minnesota, for our discussions of the pre-quantum states.

Many thanks to all my friends, who kept urging me to write this book, starting with Lee Sannella, M.D., who arranged for the first public presentation of these ideas; to Richard Ingrasci, M.D., Eddie Hauben, Bill and Tom Hickey, and the rest of my friends at "Interface," who kept things moving. To my friends at Whitewood-Stamps, Jessica Lipnack, Tom Nickel, Jeff Stamps, and Frank White, all knowers of the relative and the absolute, who gave an initial criticism of the manuscript; to Paul Nardella, the electronics wizard, who designed and built the electronic instruments used in our measurements and experiments; to David Doner, M.D., who helped with the medical portion of the appendix; to Robert L. Schwartz, chairman, Tarrytown Conference Center, who arranged for the presentation of these ideas for criticism to a panel of scientists; and finally, to my wife Mirtala, who patiently edited, criticized, and typed the manuscript.

ITZHAK BENTOV

Illustrated by the author, except for some of the better-looking sketches, which were done by Rick Humesky of Ann Arbor, Michigan.

PUBLISHER'S NOTE

An outstanding exponent of the new science of consciousness, Itzhak Bentov touched all whom he encountered with his insightfulness and genius of expression. His untimely death in 1979 was an undeniable loss, but his vision—clearly presented and accessible in his writings—continues to illumine the forward path to higher consciousness.

CONTENTS

Dedicated to those individuals
who are trying to pull together diverse aspects
of nature into one new, meaningful whole . . .

PREFACE

It is with a great sense of pleasure that I write this preface to the first book by my remarkable friend, Itzhak Bentov, who is known to all as Ben.

Ben is an intuitive inventor without much formal education who likes to tinker about in his versatile basement laboratory seeking simple and practical solutions to complex technological problems. Presently, he spends most of his time developing a variety of medical instruments. This is how he makes his living, and he is sufficiently good at it to be in great demand by modern, specialized industries that desperately need his special brand of creativity.

On one of my visits to his home, I noticed on one of the book shelves of his rather extensive technical and scientific library a little book with a pink cover, titled *Winnie The Pooh,* tucked away between heavy books with ponderous technical titles. This may give some insight into the whimsical style used by Ben throughout this book.

His intuition led him into the regular practice of meditation about ten years ago, which, in turn, led to enhanced personal integration and internal coherence. This was followed by the design of experiential journeys into the microcosm and macrocosm of the universe; collectively, out of it all has flowed this beautiful little book. It is a really fine book, easy to read and worthy of the attention of all, old and young, who want to expand their awareness and grow in consciousness. It is also a most useful model for the development of our future science.

The present scientific establishment has grown somewhat fossilized by its current "world picture" and is locked into a view of reality that has outlived its usefulness. It has begun to limit mankind's growth and has so increased its sense of specialization, separateness, materiality, and mechanical computerlike functioning that it is in real danger of self-extermination. Its sense of wholeness and purpose has been severely fragmented as our egos have reveled in the individual power created by ownership of physical scientific knowledge. We desperately need to find a path back to wholeness!

This recent period of quantitative physical science has been extremely important to humankind's development since it has forged a clearly discernible, albeit materialistic, path through the uncharted terrain of Nature's expression. It has taught us how to perform meaningful, reproducible experiments and to build and test relevant theories about Nature. However, we have presently become so focused on this one path that we have lost the flexibility of sensing all the other possible paths of knowledge available to us in the wonderland of Nature.

We have come to think that the renowned "scientific method" is to be coldly objective about an experiment because that has been very effective for much of the past experimentation. However, the scientific method is really "to provide the necessary and sufficient protocol for anyone, anywhere, to successfully duplicate the experimental result." If this requires a positive, negative, or neutral mental or emotional bias, then so be it. As we move off the purely physical path in our future experimentation, we will need to include, clearly define, and quantitatively measure these states of bias because we shall find that the human mind and human intention alter the very substratum in which our physical laws operate.

Our physical science does not necessarily deal with reality, whatever that is. Rather, it has merely generated a set of consistency relationships to explain our common ground of experience, which is determined, of course, by the capacity and capabilities of our physical sensory-perception mechanisms. We have developed these mathematical laws based ultimately on a set of definitions of mass, charge, space, and time. We don't really know what these quantities are, but we have defined them to have certain unchanging properties and have thus constructed our edifice of knowledge on these pillars. The edifice will be stable so long as the pillars are unchanging. However, we appear to be entering a period of human evolvement in which certain qualities of the human being appear to be able to change, or deform, these basic quantities. Thus, our set of laws or consistency relationships will have to change to embrace this new experience. It isn't as if the old laws are wrong and need to be thrown out — no more than Newton was wrong when Einstein came along and showed that the laws of gravitation had to be altered when one adopted a frame of reference for observation that moved at velocities approaching the velocity of light. At this time, we are beginning to adopt new states of consciousness as reference frames for observing Nature, and thus the old laws will need to be altered to conform with the new experience, when the experiential sensing is sufficiently widespread as to constitute a common ground of experience. Along this path, humankind's view of itself, of the universe, and of the synergistic interrelationship of both is in for great changes.

There have been some small beginnings made toward a new "self image" for humankind, one that emphasizes the human wholeness and connectivity with everything around it. Everything seems to interact with everything else at many subtle levels of the universe beyond the purely physical level, and the deeper we penetrate into these other levels, the more do we realize that we are One.

This book takes a great step forward by simply articulating that fact — thus contributing to the understanding of our future development.

WILLIAM A. TILLER

STALKING THE WILD PENDULUM

INTRODUCTION

This book is the result of some living-room discussions that I had with friends over a period of time. They became more and more elaborate as topics were added to the original discussions. Eventually, my friends felt that presenting these ideas to a broader audience would be in order. Finally, I gave in to the well-intentioned nagging of my friends and put down some of these ideas on paper.

As I sat down to write, I wondered whether it was the right time to do so. The accumulation of knowledge is a continuous process, and it is difficult to say at what point one should say: "Stop here and write down whatever information has accumulated up until now." I have decided to start writing at my present level of ignorance simply because the circumstances forced me to do so. It is certain that I could describe many things better and add many new ideas if I were to start this book two or three years from now. However, I would still face the same situation because one's level of ignorance increases exponentially with accumulated knowledge. For example, when one acquires a bit of new information, there are many new questions that are generated by it, and each new piece of information breeds five or ten new questions. These questions pile up at a much faster rate than does the accumulated information. The more one knows, therefore, the greater his level of ignorance. This effect does seem to justify my decision to publish this information now.

Therefore, I do not claim that the information contained here is the final truth, but I hope that it will stimulate more thinking and speculation by future scientists and interested laymen.

Much of this information has come through intuitive insight, which is no justification, of course, for omitting a rational support for this material. When we come to the description of the "shape" of the universe and the process of its creation, however, a rational support becomes tenuous since we are dealing with material that cannot be fully supported yet by scientific facts. Here the principal guide for judging the material presented is one's intuition or subjective experience.

This book is designed for young people of all ages, by which I mean those whose imagination has not been stifled by the standard educational process. It is written for people who can still be awed by the way ants build their burrows, by the cold elegance of a snake, or the beauty of a flower. I am writing for people who can tolerate a temporary state of ambiguity, for those who can take change easily and are not afraid of handling wild ideas. Those who cannot tolerate change will drop out very quickly. Few scientists will read this book to the end. But I do hope that it will stimulate the thinking processes and implant some ideas into the minds of future scientists, those who will be at their peaks about the end of this century.

I am attempting in this book to build a model of the universe that will satisfy the need for a comprehensive picture of "what our existence is all about." In other words, a holistic model that encompasses not only the physical, observable universe that is our immediate environment and the distant universe observed by our astronomers but also other "realities" as well. Normally, we do not consider the emotional, mental, and intuitive components of our beings as "realities." I will try to persuade you that they are. The phenomena that we call "unexplained," like psychokineses (the moving of an object with the power of the mind), telepathy, out-of-body phenomena, clairvoyance, etc., can all be explained once we know the general underlying principles governing them.

Recently, there has been a great deal of controversy concerning these subjects. The majority of laymen and most scientists do not presently believe in the existence of such phenomena. Rather than getting ourselves involved in the controversy over the possibilities of telepathy, or whether one can function out of this body or not, I will try to demonstrate the underlying mechanisms and explain how these things might work. It will be left to the reader to decide whether the explanations I am suggesting make sense or not.

First, I suggest that the general underlying principle in all the phenomena mentioned above is an *altered state of consciousness*. These altered states allow us to function in realities that are normally not available to us. By "normally" I mean our usual waking state of consciousness or realities that are available to the person who can so regulate himself. I shall try to fit these realities into an orderly spectrum.

When taken together, all these realities form a large hologram of interacting fields in my model.

Most of us see the universe through a tiny window, which allows us to see just a single color, or reality, out of the endless spectrum of realities. Viewing our universe through this tiny window forces us to see the world in a sequential form, that is, as events that follow each other in time. This is not necessarily so.

The concept of a "model," as I am using it here, generally implies a theoretical construct that fits as many of the known facts as one has available into a neat, elegant, and compact package. A good model will also allow the prediction of the behavior of elements or components of this structure. This is a good test for the validity of the model. Also, it is nice to have a model that does not violate any presently accepted physical laws, so as not to step on anyone's toes or cause any hassles. I believe that the model I am introducing complies with these requirements, although it comes very close to the edge of present knowledge. But then, there is nothing wrong with trying to nudge that edge a tiny bit further. But a model is a model only and not the absolute truth; therefore, it is subject to change as new information appears on the horizon. When one model does not suffice to account for all the phenomena, a new one will have to be built.

The theory of relativity emphasizes the notion that no matter what we observe, we always do so relative to a frame of reference that may differ from someone else's, that we must compare our frames of reference in order to get meaningful measurements and results about the events we observe.

The quantum theory asserts that there is no way one can measure some sets of things, like momentum and position, together very accurately; it suggests (at least in one widespread interpretation) that this is so because the consciousness of the experimenter interacts with the experiment itself. Therefore, it becomes possible that the attitude of the experimenter must also influence the outcome of any particular experiment. Now this is serious business, for unless we are able to account for and describe what consciousness is, it will always put an experiment in doubt. So the problem is: What is consciousness?

If you leaf through this book, you will see a lot of diagrams, and you may have the impression that this is a technical or even a scientific book. Well, don't worry about that. I myself am a fairly stupid fellow who could not learn any mathematics at all. In fact, my brush with academia was a rather short one: I was expelled from the kindergarten at the age of four for some alleged subversive activities and have never managed to resume normal studies since, not to mention graduating from anyplace. So my mind has remained blank and unspoiled by higher learning.

In order for us to develop a common language, I have to utilize some elementary concepts in science such as the behavior of sound and of light waves, and finally, a hologram. I have tried to make the description of this behavior as palatable as possible and as short as possible. I have to convey to you how Nature works by simple examples that will suffice perfectly to handle the final concepts. I suggest, therefore, that you bear with me for the first four chapters. Beyond that it's all downhill and fun.

After Chapter 4 things become pretty outrageous because I rush into places where even angels fear to tread. (I consider angels to be a fairly timid, unenterprising bunch.) One of the points of this book is to show that when information about subjects like poltergeist phenomena, psychokinesis, ESP, ghosts, telepathy, psychic healing, spontaneous mystical experiences, etc., is organized into a reasonable order, we find that these phenomena are a manifestation of "consciousness" on increasingly higher levels.

I will, for example, handle reincarnation as a matter of fact, completely disregarding the great controversy that rages over the subject. There are two reasons for this: First, the simple fact that when one puts himself into the proper level of consciousness, one may obtain this information first-hand; second, we know that energy cannot be lost within a closed system. The main characteristic of the phenomenon of life is that it counteracts the general tendency of things to "run down." That is, a system containing a high degree of order will tend to run down toward a state of disorder while dissipating the availability of energy (increase in entropy).

Let us take the human body as an example. In order to keep ourselves alive, we have to eat. But what do we eat? We eat either animal, vegetable, or mineral products. But where do these come from? The vegetables or grasses take suitable minerals from the soil of our planet, *put order into them,* and organize them into molecules that are used to build live cells of the plant. Some of these cells are digestible by our digestive system, and some are not. We and other plant-eating animals eat the plant material and organize it into a more complex molecule — a protein found in meat. Man and other predators have the choice of eating directly the protein built up by the plant-eating animals.

The DNA of our chromosomes, which contain the information required to build extra copies of our bodies, are extremely stable substances. Very rarely do we find gross errors within that system. That is, we encounter few people who have two noses, three legs, etc. Our physical properties are well guarded within our chromosomes, down to the very finest detail, and a very high degree of order and stability is maintained there. This shows how life organizes random minerals into a very stable structure and maintains this order for a long period of time. (This is negative entropy.)

What happens when we die? The organizing life energy departs, and our bodies start decomposing rapidly. Our precious information-carrying proteins decompose into badly smelling substances within three days. With time, in the grave, these substances will be broken down into still simpler ones. We have returned to the planet the substances we borrowed from it.

But there is another component to life other than the physical body. We know that during our lifetime we build up and store enormous amounts of information. That information is also energy that is becoming organized. In childhood, the events that occur to us seem to be random and unconnected, a kind of fallout from the world of the grownups. As we grow up, we begin recognizing the patterns of events and their causes; in short, we *put order into them.* This order is analogous to the order the life force has put into the minerals to organize and integrate them into a living material body. During a (human) lifetime, we organize a lot of information on many levels. Emotional information is built up, mental information is built up, etc. This information bundle is not material, although some will say that it is the brain that contains it. What we have here is a "body" of information. It is a nonmaterial entity containing all the knowledge that we have accumulated over a lifetime, including our personality traits and character. It is the nonmaterial "us."

In life we deal, therefore, with two organizing systems, one material and one nonmaterial. At the time of death, the physical system decays, and disorder sets in; will the same thing happen to the nonphysical energy system? This system, which I shall call the "psyche," is the organizer and processor of this information, and that information is stored outside our physical bodies. I assert that the psyche can exist independent of the physical body, that this thinking and knowing part of us is conserved. It is nonphysical and therefore not subject to decay after the death of the physical body. This "body" of information will eventually be absorbed in the large reservoir of information produced by all mankind, which I shall call the "universal mind." However, this will occur over a very long period of time. It may take many thousands or millions of years for this to happen. Thus, nothing is lost. The physical body is reabsorbed by the planet, and the "body" of information is also absorbed back whence it came. No organized energy is ever lost. An experiment showing the independence of the psyche from the physical body is described in Chapter 4.

In short, I suggest that people having problems with accepting the concept of reincarnation consider this bundle of organized information as having continuity in time, while the physical body serves as just a temporary vehicle for the psyche. When the psyche, after having been without a physical body for a while (the period after death), decides that it needs additional pieces of information obtainable only through the physical body, it will acquire one and continue to associate with the new body until it wears out and dies.

Nature, as I hope to show later, needs all this information, which is organized energy, and will not allow it to go to waste. It will be stored in Nature's large information-storage hologram: the universal mind. Normally, we have no recollection of previous lives due to a self-protective mechanism similar to that which prevents us from bringing up material buried deep in our subconscious.

While in the last few years we have been witnessing a great increase in the area of psychic phenomena, still the majority of people suffer from what one may call the "giraffe syndrome," which goes as follows: One nice day an elderly resident of the Bronx decides to visit the zoo. As he walks along, admiring all the unusual animals, he suddenly finds himself staring at a set of very tall legs. As he lifts his eyes, he finds the belly of the animal connecting those legs; he keeps looking up, and all he sees is neck, neck, and more neck, and then, somewhere up in the clouds, a head. "No," he says, "this is impossible. There is no such animal." And with that he turns away from the giraffe and walks calmly on, not casting even a single glance back at it.

Most people have the giraffe syndrome when it comes to those controversial areas. Especially so affected are scientists, with the exception of a very few pioneering spirits. The problem is that they view reality through a tiny window, and they like to stay within the frame of that window. They decide that if the giraffe is too big for their window, then it's too bad for the giraffe; as far as they are concerned, it is nonexistent. Fortunately, the levels of consciousness into which I divide the different phenomena are easily available, so that anyone who is willing to spend the time and effort does not need to rely on my description of things. He can go to the zoo and see things for himself.

I must apologize to women readers for calling the Creator "He." A Creator is neither He nor She but both. But somehow I couldn't bring myself to call Him "Chairperson of the Universe." I don't think He would go for that, nor could I face Him in good conscience afterward.

1. SOUND, WAVES AND VIBRATION

We are constantly surrounded by sound. We even have a highly specialized opening in our heads for making sounds that may be meaningful to other people. We communicate through sound; in fact, it is our major means of communication. When we disturb the air in any way, we create sound. The slightest motion of our bodies disturbs the air around us, and we produce sound. When we raise our hand, we compress the air in its way, and that compressed air front will travel away from us at the speed of sound, which in air is about 740 miles per hour. When we make periodic movements with our hand, the sound becomes a note. By sound we mean here any random acoustical disturbance that may be composed of many different frequencies. A note, on the other hand, is a sound of a single frequency. We call this kind of sound "infrasound," that is, sound below our level of perception. However, when a fly or a mosquito beats its wings, it does it fast enough, and we sure can hear it. The rapid flapping of its wings produces evenly spaced compressions and rarefications of the air that become audible to us. In short, a fly or a mosquito is producing a sound or a note.

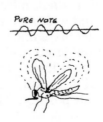

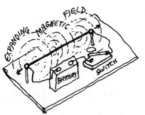

Fig. 1

Let us try to make sound in a less obvious way. We shall take a short piece of wire, connect both its ends to a battery through a switch (Fig. 1) and close the switch.

We were told in school that three things happen: (1) that electrical current will run from one side of the battery to the other; (2) that a magnetic field perpendicular to that current will shoot out and expand all the way to infinity at the velocity of light, which is about 186,000 miles per second; and (3) that the wire will heat up slightly. They probably did not tell us: (4) that when the wire heats up, it expands, and by so doing it will clearly force the air out of its way and make a kind of sound; or (5) that as the mass of the wire is accelerated in this way, it will produce gravitational waves since any time a mass is accelerated, it will broadcast gravitational waves, which will again expand to infinity at the velocity of light.

Some will say that the gravitational waves will certainly be almost infinitesimally weak. But that does not worry us as long as they are there. So our action of closing the switch has been broadcast, theoretically at least, to the outer limits of the atmosphere around the earth due to the movement of the air and was broadcast all the way to the end of the universe by the expansion of the magnetic field around the wire and by the gravitational wave due to the wire's acceleration.

The purpose of this example is to show how, in principle, even our smallest, most insignificant actions will be broadcast far and wide and thus influence something or someone — whether that something or someone is aware of it or not.

We should look now at other effects of sound. If we stretch a string on a frame (Fig. 2A), then pluck the string in the middle of its length, we shall see the outline of the string in the extreme positions of its movement; it forms two symmetrical arcs, as shown. If we pluck the string at the one-quarter mark of its length, we shall see a shape as in Figure 2B. These are *standing waves*. We get such waves only when plucking the string at distances that will divide the string into integral numbers. In Figure 2A, the frame length corresponds to half a wave, while in Figure 2B the frame accommodates a full wavelength. In Figure 2B, the string has a point in the middle at which the string is at rest and two more points at which it is attached to the frame. Such points of rest are called *nodes*. All the other points of the string are vibrating up and down. When the nodes along the string appear stationary and fixed while the rest of the string is vibrating, we call such a behavior a "standing wave."

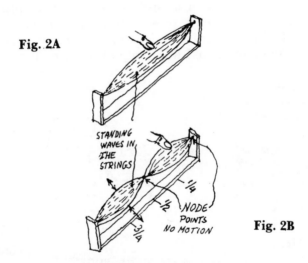

Fig. 2A

Fig. 2B

Suppose we now take a thin sheet of metal (Fig. 3), clamp it at one edge so that it stays in a horizontal position, spread some dry sand evenly over this sheet, then take a violin bow and draw it over one of the free edges of the sheet until it emits a note. Very soon we shall see that the sand grains are collecting on the sheet in a symmetrical pattern. As we apply the bow at different points along the edge of the metal, we shall get different and quite beautiful patterns on the sheet.

The reason for this aggregation of sand grains is that we are setting up the so-called standing waves in the metal. These standing waves in the metal sheet are a two-dimensional version of the standing wave in the string. These standing waves have active areas that vibrate up and down and other areas or nodes that are quiescent. The sand grains will move away from the vibrating areas and accumulate in the quiescent areas. The sand grains like to be left in peace, and they will go to the quiet, low-energy places. This pattern in sand actually outlines for us the pattern of standing waves in the metal sheet. The standing waves automatically divide the length and width of the plate into an *integral* number of half wave-lengths (Fig. 4). It is only then that a standing wave can be sustained. This is so by definition. Standing waves cannot exist unless they divide their medium into an *integral number of half waves*. A standing wave having a fractional wavelength cannot be sustained.

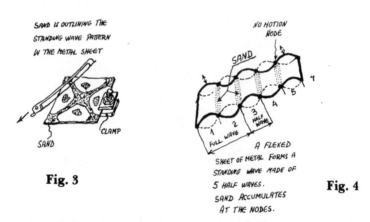

Fig. 3

Fig. 4

We can also put it another way: The dimensions of the plate are the factors that govern what is the size or wavelength of the standing wave that can be sustained in the plate. When a structure is in resonance (which means that it vibrates at a frequency that is natural to it and is most easily sustained by it), it implies the presence of a standing wave.

Let us see if we can visualize this kind of behavior in three dimensions. We could take a transparent box (Fig. 5), fill it with a fluid, and disperse particles in it with the same specific gravity as the fluid so that they stay dispersed in the fluid and do not sink to the bottom. Then, by vibrating the walls of this box from all six sides in a synchronous manner, we could cause these particles to aggregate in a symmetrical three-dimensional pattern. This pattern will look just like a highly enlarged crystal if we assume that the aggregated lumps are analogous to the atoms in a crystal. We have again produced a standing wave pattern in this box, which is a three-dimensional analog of the standing wave in the string and the metal plate. At the same time we have produced a three-dimensional object analogous to a basic building block in Nature and a highly ordered crystal — and we have done this simply by applying *sound* to an amorphous, disorganized suspension of particles.

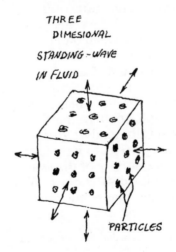

Fig. 5

In the box we have set up an interference pattern of standing waves (which we will soon explain) that governs the position of the particles. In short, by using sound, *we have introduced order* where previously there was none. It may occur to us that a crystalline structure may be seen as representing sound interacting in a volume. Is it possible that the orderly pattern of atoms in matter is the result of the interaction of some kind of "sound waves" in matter?

ICE SHEET

Fig. 6

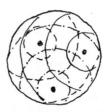

Superposed Sounds

Now let us go one step beyond and see whether "sound" can also be used for storing information or knowledge. A shallow round pan and three pebbles are all we need for this experiment. Fill the pan with water. Now drop in the three pebbles simultaneously, as shown in Figure 6, and watch the ripples spread in the pan. Each pebble is the source of waves spreading evenly across the pan. (Let us neglect the wavelets reflected back from the walls of the pan.) These waves cross each other and create quite a complex pattern of wavelets on the surface of the water. They look pretty chaotic to us. There is, however, an order in this apparent chaos. All that has happened is that the wave produced by each individual pebble expanded and reached the edge of the pan. In so doing, the waves have crossed and interacted with each other on the way to the edges of the pan. This interaction* created a complex pattern that is called an *interference pattern*. If we carefully analyze this pattern, however, we can trace back each wavelet to its source, the pebble. Let us now quick-freeze the surface of the water in the pan and lift out the resulting rippled sheet of ice. We are holding in our hands a record of the interference pattern of waves, or we may even call it a *hologram*.†

---

* Superposition is included in the broader term of "interaction."

† A hologram is usually a flat photographic film on which information is recorded about the shape of the object in the form of a wave-front interference pattern. When this film is illuminated with the same light under which the information was originally recorded, the wave front is reconstructed, and the image appears in space as a three-dimensional object, identical in "shape" to the original object. See Kock, Winston E., *Lasers and Holography*. New York: Doubleday-Anchor, 1969; London: Heinemann Educ., 1972.

Interference patterns and beat frequencies

In order to clarify what an interference pattern is, we have to learn two additional properties of sound in its different forms: (1) constructive and destructive interference; and (2) beat frequencies.

Let us take the first one. In Figure 7A, you will see what happens when two wave patterns of identical frequency and amplitude, or wavelength, meet. Let's try to superimpose them on each other. In Figure 7A, we see that the hills and valleys of the frequencies in Rows **a** and **b** match each other. If we superimpose them by measuring their heights or amplitudes from their respective baselines, then we find that hill matches hill, and valley matches valley. And when added up, they produce a wave form twice the height of the original wave forms, as shown in Row **c**. This is known as *constructive interference* because it builds up the amplitude.

If we now look at Figure 7B, we find that hills match valleys, and valleys match hills. And if we add them up, we shall find that they cancel each other out, as the flat line in Row **c** indicates. This is known as *destructive interference*. This is what is happening in our pan of water. If we look at the ripples in the ice sheet, we shall find that where hill meets hill, we end up with a hill double the original wave height, and where hill meets valley, we find just a flat spot. This is the nature of an interference pattern. However, many forms of interference patterns are possible. We may have them in a single dimension — as when we vibrate a string — or in two dimensions — as in our flat pan; or in three dimensions — as in our box in Figure 5.

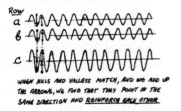

Row
a
b
c

WHEN HILLS AND VALLEYS MATCH, AND WE ADD UP
THE ARROWS, WE FIND THAT THEY POINT IN THE
SAME DIRECTION AND REINFORCE EACH OTHER

Row
a
b
c   RESULTANT = STRAIGHT LINE

WHEN HILLS AND VALLEYS OPPOSE EACH OTHER,
THE ARROWS POINT IN OPPOSITE DIRECTIONS.
THEY CANCEL EACH OTHER WHEN ADDED UP

Fig. 7A   **Fig. 7B**

Beat frequencies

Now that we know what an interference pattern is, it will be relatively easy to understand a beat frequency. In Figure 7C we see a frequency in Row **a** — let's say it is 50 cycles per second — and a frequency in Row **b** — which let's say is 60 cycles per second. If we add them up as we did before, we shall discover an interesting phenomenon. Row **c** shows the result of adding the two frequencies. What we see is a pearl-shaped wave form superimposed on top of our **a** and **b** wave forms. The reason for this becomes obvious if we examine Figure 7C carefully. Starting from the left, we see that in Row **c** the amplitude (wave height) is low where the hills and valleys oppose each other and high where both wave forms coincide or reinforce each other, which results in constructive interference. The wave patterns are said then to be *in phase*, to use a technical term.

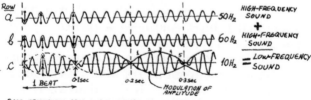

BEAT FREQUENCIES ARISE DUE TO PERIODIC CONSTRUCTIVE AND
DESTRUCTIVE INTERFERENCE BETWEEN TWO FREQUENCIES

Fig. 7C

Now, as we move to the right, we notice that the **a** and **b** waves gradually go out of phase, and the hills start facing the valleys, thus opposing each other, which means that a destructive interference is occurring. This destructive interference reaches its maximum in every fifth cycle, forming a narrow "waist" in the amplitude or "volume" of the sound at those points.

The pearly pattern in Row **c** will therefore be a "modulation" of the basic sound, which has a fixed amplitude. Modulation means a change that is being caused in an otherwise smooth or even behavior. In our case, it means an increase and a decrease of the amplitude or "volume" of the 60 and 50 cycle, per second sound. This modulation will occur 10 times per second with minima occurring every six cycles.

This 10 H.* modulation is called a beat frequency and is the difference between the **a** and **b** frequencies, or 60 Hz. minus 50 Hz. = 10 Hz. Were we to make **a** a 10 cycles per second sound and **b** a 12 cycles per second sound, we would then have a 12 minus 10 = 2 cycle per second beat frequency superimposed on these two basic frequencies. The knowledge of these two properties of "sound" will be important toward the end of this book. Note that the difference between the two fast frequencies produces a third frequency that is much slower than the first two. This, then, is a beautiful device for converting high frequencies to low ones.

Nature's information storage

Let's go back now to the sheet of ice we lifted from the pan and find a proper light source to illuminate it (Fig. 8). We shall find to our great surprise that we can see the three pebbles suspended in midair if we look through the ice toward the light. They will look very three-dimensional to us. This is a totally unexpected result. It seems that the rippled surface of the ice, or the interference pattern, has somehow *stored the information* about the whereabouts and the shape of the pebbles. The ice surface acted as a distorted lens in such a way as to focus the light to points taken up by the pebbles that have caused all these ripples. The chaotic-looking ice surface is actually an information-storage device.

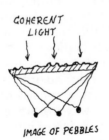

COHERENT LIGHT

COHERENT LIGHT

IMAGE OF PEBBLES   **Fig. 8**

IMAGE OF PEBBLES   **Fig. 9A**

* One cycle per second is expressed in technical language as 1 hertz, abbreviated 1 Hz.

Suppose now that due to a momentary gap in attention or plain clumsiness, this ice sheet slips out of our hands, drops on the floor, and breaks. We sadly collect the pieces, but before throwing them all out, we hold up one of them and illuminate it the same way as we did the large sheet. To our great surprise, we find the three pebbles again projected in midair (Fig. 9A). But how come?

You may remember that the information about the whereabouts of each pebble was carried by the waves moving to the edge of the pan. We know if we drop just a single pebble into the pan, it would be very easy for us to locate it. We would simply seek out the centre of the concentric wave rings or wave fronts. We know also that the waves from each pebble crossed the face of the whole pan; naturally, they must have interacted with each other across the whole surface of the pan on every square centimeter of its surface. We can show it like this: The arcs created by each pebble are crossing a small piece of the surface, and each arc can be traced back to its origin (Fig. 9B). This is the basic principle of the hologram. However, I would not recommend that you actually try to perform the experiment just described. It will not work in practice for certain complicated technical reasons, which we shall bypass. But it is perfectly useful for the purpose of explaining the workings of the most exciting information-storage device, the hologram. It is nature's way of storing information. There is already evidence that our brains store information in a holographic form. This kind of storage device is the most compact known in Nature. An example of this is the genetic code carried in our chromosomes. Each cell in our bodies carries all the information required to make an additional copy of our bodies.

Our success in storing information in the system just described depends, naturally, on the predictable and orderly behavior of the waves in the pan. They must be consistent both in velocity and in distance between the waves or wavelengths. This is what makes them reliable as carriers of information; otherwise, all we would get is a hodgepodge of waves. Here is where coherency comes in.

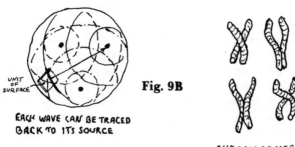

Fig. 9B

UNIT
OF
SURFACE

EACH WAVE CAN BE TRACED
BACK TO ITS SOURCE

CHROMOSOMES

Coherency

It would be good at this point to describe the way a real holo-gram is made so that you become familiar with this import-ant concept.

By *coherency* we mean an order of a certain kind. In this case, we shall talk about coherent light, without which a good hologram cannot be made. The most popular source of coherent light is a laser. The first important aspect of laser light is that it produces light of a single frequency. We all know that our sun sends us light that can be broken down by a prism into a spectrum containing all the colors of the rainbow. A laser produces light of just a single color from that rainbow, which we call "monochromatic light." In addition, the light emitted by the laser is coherent, or goes in step. By that we mean that all the light coming out of the source is moving forward in even, flat fronts (Fig. 10). This makes it possible for the laser light to stay in a narrow beam over very large distances.

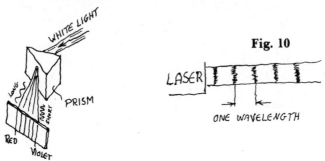

WHITE LIGHT

PRISM

RED

VIOLET

Fig. 10

LASER

ONE WAVELENGTH

There is a better way to describe coherency. Suppose we have a parade and a company of soldiers marching in military fashion down a main street. They are moving along, ten abreast, very carefully aligned in each row. The distances between the rows are fixed, which is analogous to the even distances between the crests of light waves. That they are carefully aligned abreast, none of them sticking out of the line, is analogous to the light being in phase or "in step." In short, the row of soldiers is analogous to the light emitted by the laser beam. Suppose now that a slip-up occurs, and one of the soldiers, not watching his fellows, shifts out of his row, moves forward, and steps on the heel of the fellow in front of him. The latter panics, thinking that he is lagging behind, and he jumps forward and bumps into the fellow ahead of him. Now this starts a general panic in which soldiers bumping into each other disrupt the nice even width of the moving column. The neat column diverges, broadens, then opens up completely in great disorder in spite of the fact that their commander is blowing his whistle, tearing at his hair, and using strong language to get his men back into line. What we have learned from this disastrous parade is that a beam of light can stay in a narrow beam similar to a laser's beam only as long as it is coherent. When coherency is lost, the beam will tend to expand rapidly just as will the beam of a regular flashlight.

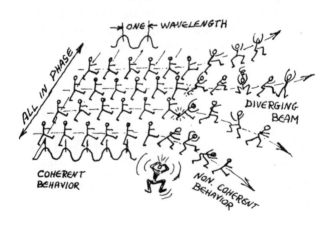

The hologram

We have seen before that information can be stored by an interference pattern of waves. To have interference, we must have at least *two interacting components,* and here is how it is done (Fig. 11):

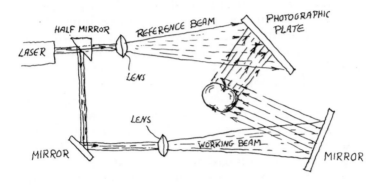

Fig. 11

The laser light beam is split into two components by a half mirror, that is, a semi-transparent mirror. This allows part of the beam to continue undisturbed while part of it is deflected to another mirror. Both narrow beams are spread open by lenses. The upper beam, which we shall call the *reference beam,* arrives at a photographic plate after an eventless flight, since no event of note has occurred on its way to the plate. It proceeds then to deposit its imprint on the film.

The other half of the beam we shall call the *working beam.* This beam's trip had an event: It had encountered on its way an object, in this case an apple, that it had illuminated and with which it had interacted. (We don't consider encounters through mirrors and lenses as worthwhile talking about.) The working beam will then be reflected from the apple and fall on the film. There it will meet its twin, the reference beam, and will tell it all about its experiences with the apple. (Neither of them suspect that their interaction is being recorded on film.) The interaction between the two beams will cause ripples to form between them, which will form the interference pattern we are already familiar with since the light waves will behave in this case the same way as do water waves. However, these ripples do not at all resemble the shape of the apple, but as we already know, the ripples in the photographic emulsion do contain information, and that information can be elicited from the film by illuminating the exposed film with the same light used in making the hologram. As we do that, we shall see the apple appear suspended in midair and looking very three-dimensional and real. We could be easily deceived, when viewing an image reconstructed from a hologram, that we were seeing the actual object.

Note that the important part of holographic image making is the interaction of a reference beam — a beam that is pure, virgin, and untouched — with a working beam, which has had some experiences in its life. The magnitude of these experiences is being measured against the reference beam, which serves as a baseline for comparison.

Our whole reality is constructed by constantly making such comparisons. Our senses, which describe our reality to us, are making these comparisons all the time. Unfortunately, our senses, having no absolute reference line, must generate their own relative reference line. But whenever we perceive something, we always perceive differences only.*

It would be useful to take one example from Nature to see how such differences are put to use in a very obvious way. Take the bat, for instance. We all know that this little mouselike fellow lives on insects he catches in flight. Since he is

HOLOGRAM OF
AN APPLE

RECONSTRUCTED
THREE-DIMENSIONAL
IMAGE
OF THE APPLE

* Whether it be heat or cold, light or darkness, quiet or noise we always compare two relative quantities. We have no absolute measure of anything as far as our daily reality is concerned.

active at night, he has developed a sonarlike device* that serves him very well and enables him to make a reasonably easy living. He has highly specialized structures in his head that allow him to emit a very high frequency sound and to direct it in a fairly narrow beam. This is his reference beam. As this beam encounters a flying insect, some of this sound will be reflected back to the bat (Fig. 12). He picks up this echo, or we can call it the working beam, and compares it to his original squeak or chirp. There will be a difference between the two (called the Doppler effect), and this difference tells the bat how far away the insect is and how fast it is flying, relative to him. As the bat successfully closes in on the insect, the difference between the two frequencies — the emitted frequency and the echo — diminishes. When it becomes very small, the bat opens its mouth and swallows the echo. Some echoes, as the bat surely knows, are tastier than others.

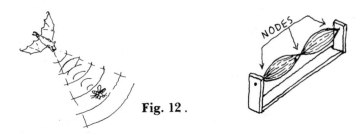

Fig. 12 .

We see now that by appreciating the *difference* between two sounds or vibrations, one can get along quite well in life. There are many creatures that make a living by appreciating differences in sound: porpoises, whales, and many others. We humans also utilize this technique in less obvious ways in color vision, hearing, etc.

Oscillators and resonant systems

We may describe an oscillator as any object that moves in a regular, periodic manner. We may call a vibrating string an

* Sonar: an underwater sound-detection device.

oscillator, or a weight hanging from a spring, or a pendulum — anything that performs a repetitive, periodic movement, that is, vibrates. We may generalize and say that oscillators produce a sound or a note, whether audible or not, as long as they alter their environment in a *periodic* manner. That environment may be tissue, as in the heart-aorta oscillating system, water, air, electrical fields, gravitational fields, or anything else.

Suppose we tune two violins, then put one of them on the table and play a note on the other. If we watch carefully, we shall see that the same string that we are playing on one violin is also humming on the violin that we placed on the table. Clearly, there is a "sympathetic resonance" between the two. Let us analyze what is happening.

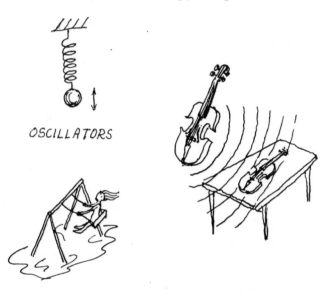

OSCILLATORS

When we draw the bow over a string, it vibrates at its own natural frequency, which we call self-frequency. Since the two violins are correctly tuned, we know that the natural frequencies of both strings were identical. Within a system like this (we shall call the two violins a "system"), it is very easy to transfer energy. In this case, we are talking about acoustical energy. The air waves generated by the first violin impinge on the second violin. The string that is tuned to the emitted note will absorb the energy of the waves of that frequency preferentially because that energy comes to it at its own natural frequency. The energy transfer within this system is therefore optimum, and such a system, made up of two *tuned oscillators,* is called a resonant system.

Let us take another example. Suppose we get several old-fashioned pendulum-type grandfather clocks. Let us hang them on a wall and arrange their pendulums so that they will start out beating each at a different angle, that is, out of phase with each other. In a day or two, we shall find that all the pendulums are beating in phase, as if locked together. (Pendulum length should be the same for all of them.) Here we see that the tiny amount of energy that was transmitted through the wall from clock to clock was sufficient to bring them into phase with each other. If we disturb one of the clocks, it will get locked into rhythm quite fast. The larger the number of oscillators within such a system, the more stable the system, and the more difficult it is to disturb. It will force a wayward oscillator back into line very quickly.

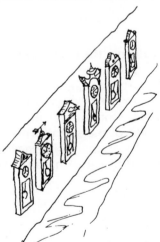

The sound of the body

The heart is a big noisemaker. We can easily check this by putting our ear on someone's chest and listening to it. Each beat shakes the whole body, and the body has a typical response to this beat, which is quite easily measured. Figure 13 shows what such motion looks like when measured with a sensitive seismographlike instrument.* This movement is clearly related to the heart heat; in fact, the largest peak we see in this graph is caused by the ejection of blood from the heart's left ventricle. The portion between the large peaks looks fairly irregular and is caused by the vibration of the body due to the action of the blood in the aorta, which is the largest artery in our body. This irregular portion is due to a destructive interference pattern set up in the aorta, as will be shown later.

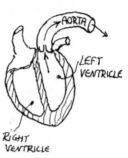

When we stop breathing, the irregular signal in Figure 13 turns into a nice, regular, practically sine-wave pattern (Figure 14). This is surprising, and when we look into the reasons for this behavior, we find that the heart-aorta system has become a so-called resonant system, as shown in Figure 15, in which the length of the aorta forms one-half a wavelength of this system. By resonant system we mean that it resonates just like a tuned musical instrument.

| Fig. 13 | Fig. 14 |

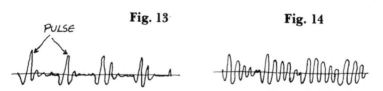

* A seismograph is an instrument used to measure tremors of the earth's crust during earthquakes.

Here is what seems to be the case: When the left ventricle of the heart ejects blood, the aorta, being elastic, balloons out just beyond the valve and causes a pressure pulse to travel down along the aorta (Fig. 16). When the pressure pulse reaches the bifurcation in the lower abdomen (which is where the aorta forks in two to go into the legs), part of the pressure pulse rebounds and starts travelling up the aorta. If in the meantime the heart ejects more blood, and a new pressure pulse is travelling down, these two pressure fronts will eventually collide somewhere along the aorta and produce an interference pattern. This is reflected in the movement of the body and is the reason for the irregular pattern of body motion in Figure 13.

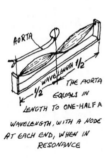

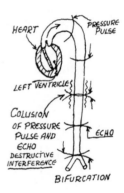

Fig. 15   **Fig. 16**

However, when the breathing stops, it looks as if some communication has been set up between the heart and the bifurcation. Some kind of a signal seems to travel from the bifurcation to the heart, saying to it: "Heart, 'hold it.' Hold your next pulse until the echo from the bifurcation returns to you — only then should you eject the next quantity of blood." When this happens, and the echo and pulse move out of the heart together, and they continue to move up and down in synchrony, then such a system is said to be in resonance. It causes the body to move harmoniously up and down about seven times a second, hence the nice, regular, large-amplitude sinewave pattern in Figure 14. The amplitude or height of this signal is about three times the average of the normal signal. Another characteristic of resonant behavior is that it requires for its sustenance a minimum amount of energy.

Well, but how long can we hold our breath? Certainly, not over a minute or so comfortably, and so we start breathing and ruin the nice rhythmic pattern. Let us not forget now that our body includes our head, and inside the skull, carefully packaged, is a very delicate instrument: the brain. This brain is cushioned by a thin layer of fluid and is wrapped in a tight bag, the dura. About the simplest way to visualize this system is to have a relatively soft, round fruit, such as a peach, enclosed in a can containing a heavy syrup. If we shake the can, we find that the peach will hit the top and the bottom of the can and be accelerated with a small delay in the direction in which the can is moving. This movement is quite small, only .005 to .010 mm. This is exactly what happens to the brain.

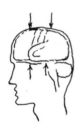 

The question is: How come we are not aware of this happening to us? It's probably because when something is happening to the nervous system for an extended period of time, and that event is not traumatic, it will not be brought to our conscious attention because the portion of the brain that is in charge of censoring and separating meaningful signals from unmeaningful ones will relegate it to the heap of unimportant signals, which require no conscious processing. We know from experience that we can easily get used to and disregard the loud ticking of a clock next to us or the noise in the cabin of an airplane.

The noise is, however, filed away somewhere and affects us in some subtle ways. If we were to ask the brain how it would like to be treated — whether shaken at a random, irregular rate or in a rhythmic, harmonious fashion — we can be sure that the brain, or for that matter the whole body, would prefer the latter.

Rhythm entrainment

Suppose we go out on a balmy summer evening and notice some fireflies settling in a bush, blinking off and on. At first, this blinking is random, but fairly soon we notice that an order is slowly developing. After a while, we see that the fire-flies in the whole bush are blinking on and off in unison. This phenomenon is called *rhythm entrainment*. It seems that nature finds it more economical in terms of energy to have periodic events that are close enough in frequency to occur in phase or in step with each other. That is the mean-ing of rhythm entrainment.

Let us take another example. When electronic circuits are built so that they contain oscillators (of electronic type com-mon in radio or TV circuits) that happen to oscillate in fre-quencies that are close enough to each other, there will be a tendency of the oscillators to get locked in step with each other and oscillate at the frequency of one of them. Usually, it is the fastest oscillator that will force the slower ones to operate at this pace. Here again, Nature feels that it is more economical if two or any number of oscillators that vibrate at frequencies close enough to each other work together rather than insist on keeping their small differences.

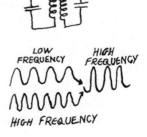

LOW
FREQUENCY

HIGH
FREQUENCY

HIGH FREQUENCY

Major effects of rhythm entrainment occur in Nature. Our biological rhythms are entrained by light and to a certain extent by gravitational effects. These are the two most obvious factors. However, magnetic, electromagnetic, atmospheric, and subtle geophysical effects influence us in ways that are not presently well understood. We usually get up with daylight and go to sleep at night. The sleep-wake cycles of animals and birds are more strongly tied to the light-dark cycle than those of our "civilized" humanity because we have developed artificial sources of light and can change our light-dark cycle at will. However, we all know that when our light-dark cycle, which runs our biological clocks, is drastically altered, as when we take a long jet flight in an east-west direction and cross several time zones, such an interference with our biorhythm has quite a marked effect on our ability to function in the new environment for a day or two.

An interesting experiment was performed by Professor Frank Brown, Jr., of Northwestern University, Evanston, Illinois.* In order to check out what factors influence the biorhythm of animals, he had some live oysters shipped to his lab from the Long Island Sound, a distance of about a thousand miles in a east-west direction. These oysters open and close their valve in rhythm with the tides. The animals were shipped in tight opaque containers filled with sea water. Upon arrival, they were stored in a lab with no natural daylight. On first examination, the oysters, geared to the rhythm of tides in the Long Island Sound, kept opening and

* Gauquelin, Michel. *The Cosmic Clocks.* Chicago: Regnery, 1974; London: Peter Owen, 1969.

closing their valves. In about two weeks, they started shifting their rhythm, and a while later, they stabilized in a rhythm that coincided with the passage of the moon over Evanston, Illinois. In this case, we may assume that the oysters are indeed rhythm-entrained by the gravitational effects of the moon.

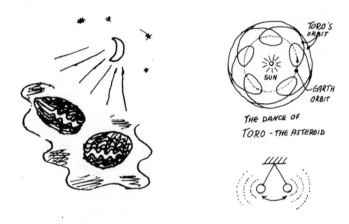

THE DANCE OF
TORO - THE ASTEROID

However, it is not only we, the tiny creatures of this planet, who are rhythm-entrained. The big and mighty asteroids and the planets themselves are rhythm-entrained and develop resonances in their orbits as they rotate about the sun. Asteroids, which are minor planets, will not only respond to the gravitational pull of the sun but will also be strongly affected by the gravitational fields of the major planets. They must dance, so to speak, to the tune of two masters, and so the asteroids develop little dances to the music of the spheres in which they pay tribute to the forces involved. They go into resonant orbits and describe minor loops around the planets within their major loop around the sun.

All the phenomena described in this chapter are of a periodic, repetitive nature. We have made a generalization at the beginning, saying that when such a rhythmic movement occurs, it affects its environment, whether that environment is air, water, solids, electromagnetic or gravitational fields. In the case of air, water, or a solid, these vibrations will affect our near environment only and can be called "sound." If we shake our electromagnetic or gravitational fields, the disturbance in the environment will travel faster and farther. We will still apply the word "sound" to it, although it will be a sound of a different kind since it would travel at the velocity of light. We could actually associate our whole reality with sound of one kind or another because our reality is a vibratory reality, and there is nothing static in it. Starting with the nucleus of an atom, which vibrates at enormous rates, the electrons and the molecules are all associated with characteristic vibratory rates. A most important aspect of matter is vibratory energy.

When we think, our brains produce rhythmic electric currents. With their magnetic components, they spread out into space at the velocity of light, as do the electric waves or sounds produced by our hearts. They all mingle to form enormous interference patterns, spreading out and away from the planet.

They are admittedly weak, but they are there. The more finely our systems are tuned, the clearer a signal we can pick out of the general noise and jumble of "sounds." When we have a system of *tuned oscillators,* even the tiniest signal can be picked up. You may recall that it requires very little energy of the correct frequency to drive a resonant system.

Our planet itself is producing shock waves in the plasma*

* Plasma refers here to a tenuous gas containing charged particles.

that fills the solar system. These shock waves interact with those caused by other planets and produce resonances between the planets and the asteroids. In short, our whole reality is based on one common factor, and that is periodic change, or sound. Our senses are geared to respond to all these different "sounds," but we are always comparing one sound with another. We can appreciate only *the differences in sound.*

Summary

We have seen various ways of producing sound. We know that when a string or any other structure vibrates, it may develop *standing waves.* These are waves that occupy a "fixed" position in any structure, whether it is a string, a plate, a container filled with a liquid, or a blood vessel.

Nodes are the spots in which minimum motion occurs.

When sets of waves are superposed, *interference patterns* result.

A *hologram* is an interference pattern of light waves on a photographic plate.

When two differing frequencies are superposed, *beat frequencies* result.

Coherency is an in-step or in-phase behavior of waves.

Oscillators are devices that move in a periodic, repetitive fashion between two points of rest. Our bodies are also such devices.

Oscillators vibrating out of phase with each other may get locked into phase through *rhythm entrainment.*

A system of oscillators that is in phase can *resonate.*

Our reality is a vibratory reality, filled by "sounds" of different kinds.

We respond to *differences* in these sounds.

2. A LOOK THROUGH A SUPERMICROSCOPE

In the last chapter, we armed ourselves with the knowledge of sound and vibration behavior. We could put this knowledge to good use now by looking for such things as standing waves, resonances, rhythm entrainment, etc., in the live body. Suppose that we take a very special microscope, an imaginary one that can magnify so greatly that single atoms are easily observable. Let us take a look at some exposed live tissue. We are now using a low magnification; we see an irregular network of little blood vessels, pieces of connective tissue, and some muscle tissue and bone. All over this we see some blood, and the overall impression is quite an irregular and gooey mess. Let us focus now on some muscle tissue and start enlarging. The gooey muscle suddenly turns into highly organized muscle fibers, all nicely aligned. A little more magnification will show long fibers made of coiled long molecules, placed in regular arrays. With a bit more magnification we find that the gooey little piece of muscle tissue has turned into a highly ordered, practically crystalline material.* As we turn the magnification still higher, we

THE STRUCTURE
OF STRIATED
MUSCLE

COILED
MOLECULE

* Do you remember how we produced a model of a crystal in Chapter 1 by an interference pattern of sound in a box (Fig. 5)?

see little atoms vibrating in groups about their location in the long coiled molecules. Whole sections of the molecules are undulating regularly; everything is in a constant, very rapid, but very orderly motion. This vibratory motion occurs many million times a second.

If we now apply a magnet to this piece of muscle, we notice right away a very slight change in the undulation of molecular segments. If we apply an electric field, the results will be similar. We are changing the wavy motion of the molecular segments. That effect is possibly due to the fact that we have just slightly changed the orbits of the outer electrons in the atoms making up these long molecules.

Let us now magnify a piece of bone. Very soon an orderliness will emerge: highly ordered bone crystals embedded like jewels in webs of long molecular strings. Everything is vibrating. Suppose we now apply an electric field* to the bone. As soon as we do that, the crystal changes its length. It shrinks or stretches instantly in response to the field. Some more magnification will give us an even better look at this crystal: we see the atoms weaving back and forth like a field of ripe wheat blown by the wind. They move in unison and in beautiful rhythm. Acoustical energy is flowing through the crystal.

* An electric field is a region in which electrical forces are present. Such a field exerts a force on any electrically charged particle within it.

Next we focus on the atoms. At first, they appear as little shadowy balls vibrating about fixed points in the molecule. As we magnify, we see less and less. The electron shell has somehow dissolved, and we are looking at a vacuum. As we further magnify, we see something tiny moving about. We focus on what we suspect is the nucleus of the atom, located in this vast space within the atom.

If we take the diameter of the nucleus of a hydrogen atom to be 1 mm., then the diameter of the electron orbit will be about 10 meters, a ratio of 1 to 10,000, and the intervening space is vacuum.

As we zero in and further magnify the vibrating nucleus, it seems to be dissolving. We are looking at some shadowy pulsation; some more magnification, and the nucleus is almost gone. We are sensing the pulsation of some energy; it seems to be a rapidly pulsating field. But where did the bone go? We thought that we were looking at a solid piece of matter!

Well, it seems that the real reality — the microreality, that which underlies all our solid, good, common-sense reality — is made up, as we have just witnessed, of a vast empty space filled with oscillating fields! Many different kinds of fields, all interacting with each other. The tiniest disturbance in one field carries over into the others. It's an interlocked web of fields, each pulsating at their own rate but in harmony with the others, their pulsations spreading out farther and farther throughout the cosmos.

Whenever a focus of disturbance tends to drive these fields out of their harmonious rhythm, the irregularity will spread and disturb the neighboring fields. As soon as the source of disturbance is removed, orderly rhythm will return to the system. Conversely, when a strong harmonizing rhythm is applied to this matrix of interlocking fields, its harmonic influence may entrain parts of the system that may have been vibrating off key. It will put more orderliness into the system.

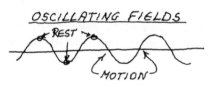

We may look at a disease as such out-of-tune behavior of one or another of our organs of the body. When a strong harmonizing rhythm is applied to it, the interference pattern of waves, which is the organ, may start beating in tune again. This may be the principle of psychic healing.

So by taking an imaginary trip into a highly magnified image of our "solid" reality, we found a new underlying reality. Our solid reality dissolved into a rapidly pulsating matrix of fields of energy, an interference pattern of waves filling the vast vacuum of our bodies and continuing beyond them in a more diluted fashion. We have also seen that the application of any kind of energy to this matrix of fields is somehow going to affect the behavior of our by now rather abstract "matter" or tissue. Whether that energy is electric, magnetic, gravitational, or acoustic, it will always interact and affect us somehow, whether it is applied from a distance or directly to our skin.

Now we may not wonder about the behavior of Dr. Brown's Long Island oysters. The gravitational changes in the field of the earth caused by the moon easily penetrate all our matter, so no wonder that they rhythm-entrained the oysters to open and close on Chicago time.

Our bodies are, of course, made up of many kinds of tissue. Certain tissues will interact more with one kind of vibratory energy than another. For instance, certain radiations will penetrate our skin to different depths. Ultraviolet rays will affect one layer of our skin and not another. They will not penetrate deeply. Sound waves will penetrate and reflect from certain tissues better than from others. The body as a whole will be affected by gravitational or magnetic effects. No matter how small the effect, our psyches may respond strongly to it. Just check police records on the effect of the full moon on the crime rate at your local police station or the incidence of violence in psychiatric wards in mental hospitals. In both instances, there is a great increase.

It seems that the full moon will have the stronger effect; the new moon, a lesser one, but both effects are above average. Earlier we discussed the rhythmic motion of our bodies and of our skulls, which accelerates our brains up and down. The force causing this acceleration is much stronger than the effect of the distant moon overhead. Still, the moon's gravitational influence tends to affect this force ever so slightly, and that influence seems sufficient to affect our psyches very strongly. Naturally, people do not react to the moon equally strongly. The strongest effect is found in highly emotional or emotionally unbalanced people.

Let us look now at the fields we encounter outside our bodies.

The electromagnetic and electrostatic fields making up and shaping our bodies are relatively strong and serve to hold our atoms and molecules together. They weaken as they move outside our bodies. We are surrounded and permeated by several fields:

1. The so-called isoelectric static field of the planet.
2. The electrostatic fields created by our bodies.
3. The magnetic field of the earth.
4. The electromagnetic field, which has a very wide spectrum, ranging from the very slow wave caused by disturbances in the atmosphere, through the spectrum of the visible light, and into the ultraviolet and higher frequency radiation.
5. The gravitational fields of the earth, the moon, and the neighboring planets and the sun.
6. The electromagnetic fields created by humans; the different broadcasting fields of radio and television networks.

We shall discuss the first two of these fields. As you know, our planet is surrounded by a layer of electrically charged particles called the ionosphere. The lower layer of the ionosphere starts at about 80 km. from the surface of the earth. It is a charged layer and is known to reflect radio waves. It is therefore essential to radio communication around the globe. We are interested, however, in another aspect of this layer.

Since this is a highly charged layer, it forms a so-called capacitor with the earth (Fig. 17). This means that there is a difference in electric potential between these two, the earth being negatively and the ionosphere positively charged. This potential difference is evenly distributed along the distance between the earth and the ionosphere and comes to

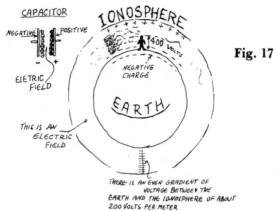

Fig. 17

about 200 volts per meter. When standing on the earth, we are moving constantly within this field, which is, so to speak, very "stiff." It means that it behaves like a fairly rigid jelly. We have all had the experience of handling a bowl of jelly and know how sensitive it is to vibration. Visualize a few raisins embedded in this jelly. Poke one of the raisins and vibrate it; you'll soon see that all the other raisins in this jelly are vibrating, too. We can also add that the raisins are quite well *coupled* with this jelly field. By coupling we mean that there is a good connection between the raisin and the jelly, that the energy transfer between them is good. They can't make the slightest movement without the jelly transmitting it to the other raisins.

The electrostatic field of the planet is like the stiff jelly. When our bodies move and vibrate, these movements are transmitted to the environment, including all human and animal bodies on this planet. These fields not only impinge on our bodies, but they also affect the charges inside our bodies. But how effective is this coupling? Can't we make

the slightest move without detection? What influences this coupling effect? The coupling is, in fact, quite good. It has been shown by our measurements that when a human body is standing on the ground under normal conditions, it is electrically grounded. It acts as a sink for the electrostatic field and will distort the force lines somewhat. But if there were a charge on our bodies, the interaction would be stronger, independent of the polarity of the charge.

It turns out that our bodies do indeed have a charge. They keep producing a field around themselves as long as they are alive. The electrostatic field of the body can nowadays be quite easily measured by commercially available static meters. We have constructed a special device in our lab to measure these fields (Fig. 18).

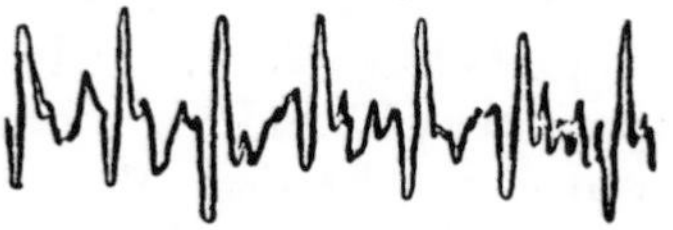

Fig. 18

Here is a reading taken by this device. We can measure the disturbance produced by our bodies in the electrostatic field.* The device is sensitive enough to be able to pick up this signal at 16 to 18 inches from the body. The large waves are again created mostly by the reaction of the body to the ejection of blood from the left ventricle.The strength of this signal changes with distance from the body. The way this changes is shown in Figure 19.

We notice that as we approach the body with the sensor, there is a gradual increase in the signal. Then suddenly at about 4 inches from the body there is a sharp increase. This increase will occur within about ¼ inch movement of the sensor. The strength of this signal depends very much on the vitality of the subject. A person brimming with energy will produce a big signal, while one whose vitality is low will produce practically no signal at all.

Thus, we have an electrostatic field around the body. This field couples us well to the isoelectric field of the planet,

---

* More correctly, this field is called an electrodynamic field caused by the motion of our bodies.

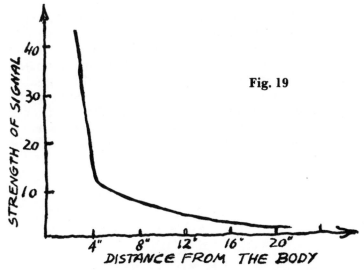

Fig. 19

which means that the motions of our bodies are transmitted far and wide around the planet. This is, naturally, a very weak signal.

Remember now the discussion about resonant systems in Chapter 1. You will recall that when we have what is called a "tuned system," consisting of at least two oscillators of identical resonant frequencies, if one of the oscillators starts emitting, the others will be activated by this signal very soon. In other words, the coupling between them is ideal. Such systems will respond to the tiniest clues and start resonating.

Remember also the case of the pendulum clocks hanging on the wall, which rhythm entrain each other. Now, you recall that the resonant frequency of the earth — ionosphere cavity — is about 7.5 cycles per second and that the micromotion of the body is about 6.8 to 7.5 Hz. This suggests a tuned resonant system. We may say now that in deep meditation the human being and the planet system start resonating and transferring energy. This is occurring at a very long wavelength of about 40,000 km., or just about the perimeter of the planet. In other words, the signal from the movement of our bodies will travel around the world in about one-seventh of a second through the electrostatic field in which we are embedded. Such a long wavelength knows no obstacles, and its strength does not attenuate much over large distances. Naturally, it will go through just about anything: metal, concrete, water, and the fields making up our bodies. It is the ideal medium for conveying a telepathic signal.

We have said previously that when we stop breathing, the amplitude of the micromotion increases by about a factor of three because the body goes into resonance, and its movement becomes very regular. Can this resonant state be extended in some way?

Meditative states

Techniques of extending this harmonious resonant state have been known for thousands of years. These are the different meditative techniques. They slow down the metabolic rate of the body so that much less oxygen is required to keep the body going. Moreover, as one becomes proficient in meditation, the breathing becomes so gentle as not to disturb the resonant state of the aorta. It seems that an automatic process develops in which the lungs and the diaphragm regulate the heart-aorta system so as to keep them well tuned and thus extend the resonant behavior in spite of some shallow breathing. The resonant state will naturally apply to the whole body. The skeleton and all the inner organs will move *coherently* at about 7 cycles per second. It so happens that the natural frequency of the normal body seems to lie in this range. It therefore takes very little effort on behalf of the heart-aorta system to drive the body at

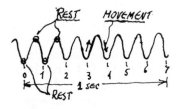

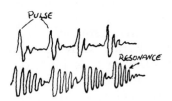

WE HAVE ABOUT FOURTEEN
PERIODS OF REST AND
FOURTEEN PERIODS OF
MOVEMENT PER SECOND

this rate. It is similar to pushing a swing in correct timing. The normally occurring destructive interference ceases, and the body starts acting in an increasingly coherent fashion.

The resonant state of the body seems to be a very restful and beneficial state. Recent scientific studies* show that the effects of meditation are not just subjective but have very marked physiological effects besides soothing jangled nerves and lowering blood pressure. It slowly but surely causes what we shall call "elevation of levels of consciousness." For different individuals this will happen at different rates. Sensitive people with delicate nervous systems will feel these effects sooner than others. However, sooner or later a large percentage of the practitioners will find that new and broad inner horizons are opening up to them, which will fill their lives to a degree they could not have imagined before. In the following chapters, more will be said about this.

But back now to the motion of the body. We have said that when a charged body is vibrating, it is coupled well to the electrostatic field of the planet. This vibration causes a regular repetitive signal or wave to propagate within this field.

* Bloomfield, Harold, et al. *TM*. New York: Delacorte Press, 1975; London: Allen & Unwin, 1976.

This signal will naturally have the tendency to entrain any "body" vibrating at frequencies close to it. In other words, if there are other people in the vicinity, or anywhere on the globe, who are meditating and are approaching this resonant frequency, they will be pushed along and locked into that frequency. We can therefore say that a nucleus of meditating body or bodies will emit a simple harmonic motion or a "sound" of approximately 7 Hz. through the electrostatic field of the planet. This emission will entrain others and help them in their effort to achieve the resonant state. The more bodies are thus locked in, the stronger the signal becomes. Due to the different time zones around the globe, there are always some people resonating and keeping this "sound" going. When in the coming chapter we learn to look at the planet as having consciousness, we will find out that it pleases the planet no end to have such an accompaniment to its tune.

Summary

When we magnify our physical matter very much, we find that we are made mostly of void permeated by oscillating fields. This is what *objective physical reality* is composed of.

This matrix of oscillating fields, which is the human body, is easily influenced by outside fields, whether natural, such as the changing low-frequency electromagnetic fields generated by weather patterns or by changing magnetic and gravitational fields affected by the moon and the sun; or it can be influenced by artificial fields produced by humans, such as broadcasting fields of radio and television networks.

Our bodies generate electrostatic fields of their own.

When in the meditative state, our bodies go into resonance with the electric field of the planet.

3. A MORSE CODE OF ACTION AND REST

You will remember from the previous chapter that our physical bodies and all matter is made up of interacting electromagnetic fields vibrating at tremendous frequencies. At room temperature an atom will vibrate at a rate of 10^{15} Hz. (That means 1 followed by fifteen zeros.) The nucleus of an atom will vibrate at about 10^{22} Hz. These are almost inconceivably fast rates. In the process of inventing live systems, Nature had to come up with sensory organs that will allow these living things to interact with their environment. It had to use available building blocks that, as we have seen, are very jittery. In order to communicate with a slow mind, Nature has largely given up the tremendous information-handling capacity that is inherent in matter itself. If an atom is vibrating a million billion times a second (10^{15} Hz.), that means that it occupies two distinct states, so many times a second. In other words, it can say, for instance, "Yes, no, yes, no," so many times a second. Now if we can utilize all this capability by superimposing a modulation on this fast behavior that would in turn alter this behavior either in amplitude or frequency, we would have a very fast communication device. This speed is utilized in molecular interactions, but our sense organs are hopelessly slow to handle directly the onslaught of this much information.

Well, after a lot of experimentation, Nature came up with a reasonable solution. It has bound atoms into molecules, which have much lower vibratory rates because of their much larger mass. Out of these molecules — which still vibrate at Gigahertz (10^9 Hz.) rates — it has made live cells, which are the building blocks of all organisms. Then came the specialized nerve cells, or neurons. A rudimentary nervous system resulted that translated sensory input into a slow Morse code fashion of *action and rest*. It was a process of gradually stepping down the high vibratory rates of the atoms, to the "reasonable" vibratory rates of the molecules, to the "acceptable" frequency response of the cells (which is in the 10^3 Hz. range) for an assembled live cell. In other words, a cell will be able to respond to stimuli at that rate.

It is very possible that sensations that do not come directly through the sense organs — such as general malaise or feelings of anxiety and doom, restlessness or elation — may come through a different kind of mechanism. These sensations might be evoked by the fluctuation of the different fields in which we are immersed and by the rate of vibration of the molecular structures in the brain or the endocrine glands.

In the last chapter, we cited the effect of the moon on emotions. Changes in the electrostatic field may also cause such effects as lassitude or elation.

The sensory organs

Our sensory system, as you may remember from biology classes, is made up of a system of sensing nerve cells located at the proper places in our sense organs. The cells are connected by long nerve filaments that join into bundles with neighboring filaments. These eventually lead to the spine to form the spinal cord, then lead up into the different areas of the brain.

Physiological studies show that when a sensory nerve cell is not stimulated, the output of that cell will consist of sparse and unevenly spaced electrical pulses or *spikes,* as they are called (Fig. 20). However, if we apply pressure or any other stimulus to that nerve cell, its output will become very lively. With each stimulus the cell will fire off salvos of closely spaced spikes. Their rate per unit time will depend on the strength of the stimulus (Fig. 21).

Fig. 20

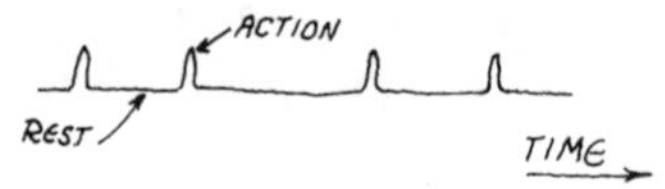

Fig. 21 ~$\frac{1}{0.1 sec}$ MMMMMMMMLLLLLLLLL

Our whole sensory system operates this way, whether it is optical input coming through the eyes, acoustical through the ears, or tactile through the skin — and the end result is a series of spikes conducted to the appropriate area in the brain. In short, our senses translate the surrounding reality to us into a *Morse code language of action and rest*. Action comes when the neuron fires its spike, and rest comes as the cell is regenerating and readying itself for the next firing. Out of this action-and-rest code our brain constructs for us, for example, the form of a rose, its texture, its color and smell — in other words, its "rosiness." Or it will construct for us a faint image of distant galaxies coming in through the eyepiece of a telescope.

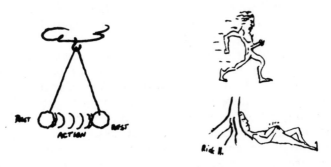

Let us see what other systems operate on an action-and-rest basis. The simplest one appears to be the pendulum. We all are familiar with the relaxed pace of the grandfather-clock pendulum, slowly moving to and fro. It is behaving in what is called by physicists "simple harmonic motion."

Let us take a weight on a string and set it in motion (Fig. 22) so that it describes a circle, which we shall call trajectory "A." This circle is connecting two points, I and II, in the plane in which the pendulum is moving. Now let us start confining the movement of the pendulum by forcing it to move between two parallel plates, which are moved closer

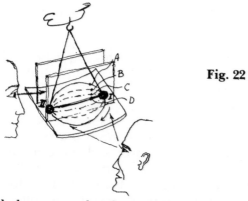

Fig. 22

and closer to each other, so that its orbit will become flattened into an ellipse. We shall call this trajectory "B." If we
confine the orbit of the pendulum even more by moving the
plates closer to each other, we get a very elongated elliptical
orbit "C," and if we continue to restrict the freedom of this
pendulum, we finally force it to move in a straight line,
which is connecting points I and II.

What we did to the unfortunate pendulum was to limit its
freedom and force it to move along one plane only. This
back-and-forth motion between two points is the equivalent
of projecting the movement of the pendulum onto a flat
screen facing the observer's eye. We have converted circular
motion into a reciprocating motion by taking away some of
the freedom of the pendulum. However, we did not change
the time required for each to-and-fro movement; it is still
keeping the correct time. All we did was to convert a simple
circular periodic motion into a linear one, which is still a
simple and harmonic motion, originally generated by a circular motion. In this way, we can convert all uniform circular motion, whether it is that of an electron or of a planet,
into a simple harmonic motion. The only limitation is that
it has to be viewed always from the same plane and the same
angle if two observers are to agree on the timing and position of the pendulum in each instance. Thus, subjectivity
enters the picture. The two extreme points of the pendulum,
at which there is no apparent motion, are different for different observers unless the event is observed from the same

angle. If the observer looks along the direction of the back-and-forth motion of the pendulum as it moves in a straight line between the plates, he will see no motion at all. He may see the pendulum slightly closer and slightly farther from himself, but no sideways motion will be visible. He will be observing the two points of rest.

Hierarchies of motion

In Chapter 2 we described the microrealities as being made up of interacting energy fields that can be represented as particles. These particles have many properties. They have a "charge," a "spin," "magnetic moment," and "strangeness," — and in the last few years "color" and "charm" have entered the picture.

Let us visualize an atom made up of a nucleus and electron shells. We find the electrons orbiting rapidly about the nucleus while at the same time rotating about their own axes. If we look now at an aggregate of atoms in a crystal, we find that they vibrate about their fixed position in the lattice of this crystal. Thus, the microlevel of Nature is represented by two kinds of motion: a circular spinlike motion and a reciprocating motion due to vibration, each about a relatively fixed point.

Let us go one step up in the hierarchy of structures in Nature, for example, to that of large molecules. These molecules confine the atoms to relatively fixed positions, and any free branches of such molecules will tend to exhibit pendulum-like movements and rotation. The free segments of these long molecules will also vibrate in and out, resembling the movement of a stretched vibrating string. The rate of these movements is much, much slower than the rate of orbiting of the electron about the nucleus.

If we look at simple living structures such as protozoa or plankton, we find only one kind of motion: the reciprocating or to-and-fro motion of the pendulum or spring. If we watch simple single-celled animals under a microscope, we find that their movements are jerky and that they derive their movements by beating their flagellae back and forth rapidly. They may rotate about their axes, but that is caused by the reciprocating action of their little "legs."* As the organism becomes more complex and a rudimentary heart develops, we find a back-and-forth pulsation of the primitive blood fluid that causes, in turn, a back and forth recoil of the body.

Throughout the animal kingdom, from plankton to elephant to humans, we find that reciprocating motion prevails. There is almost no spin in the living structures. We are confined to a pendulumlike or, if you wish, oscillating behavior.

As we go up the hierarchy of sizes and to heavenly bodies, orbiting and spin reappear. We know that all planets rotate about their axes while at the same time they orbit around their respective stars. We know that galaxies rotate, as do galactic clusters, and so on. In short, we find that one of the unique characteristics of live creatures is their reciprocating motion. But is Nature so inept that it could not invent a wheel, which our very primitive ancestors easily managed to do? How come? Or is there more to it than meets the eye?

Stalking the wild pendulum

Let us go back to the old grandfather clock with its leisurely swinging pendulum and see what is unusual about its movement. Apparently, there is nothing unusual. Its motion can be described as being made up of *motion and rest*. We recall vaguely having heard something like this before.

Let us analyze the motion of the pendulum. As it approaches its point of rest, it slows down more and more; eventually, it stops and starts moving in the opposite direction. The laws of classical mechanics tell us that at the point

* It has been shown that in some bacteriae there is indeed a rotary device present. The flagellae are attached to the body of the bacterium through a rotary joint, which is driven by a molecular rotary motor. Berg, Howard C. "How Bacteriae Swim." *Scientific American*, August 1975, pp. 36-44.

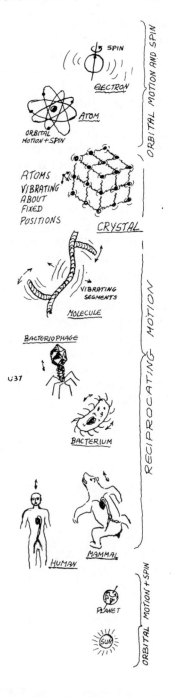

of rest the acceleration of the body is maximum; its potential energy is maximum; its velocity is zero; and the time required for changing the velocity of the pendulum is zero. If we analyze the events taking place at the zero point from the point of view of quantum mechanics, we get a different picture. Let us view the pendulum bob as a mathematical point, that is, a point that is too small to be measured (a dimensionless point) and follow its progress as it slows down. Clearly, the point will cover a smaller and smaller distance per unit time as it approaches its turning point. But quantum mechanics tell us that when distances go below Planck's distance, which is 10^{-33} cm., we enter, in effect, a new world. The causal relationship between events breaks down; movements become jerky rather than smooth. Time and space may become "grainy" or "chunky." Perhaps a piece of space can be traversed by a particle of matter in any direction without necessarily being synchronized with a piece of time. In short, a pair of events would occur in either time or space, the pair not being connected causally but by a random fluctuation. Suppose, indeed, that a material point can traverse space without necessarily requiring any chunk of time for the process. Should this happen, then a chunk of space has been spanned without any time elapsing. If we divide that tiny piece of distance to zero time, we find that the event occurred at infinite velocity. In other words, when we move through space without using up time, no matter over how short a distance, that event occurs at infinite velocity!

There is a principle in physics that states that any event that is not prohibited by the laws of physics should happen! What, then, happens to the pendulum? All the points on it behave the same way; therefore, all of it must for a tiny fraction of a second move at infinite velocity. Can a physical object move faster than the velocity of light?

Let us approach this from a different angle. We have heard about Heisenberg's principle of uncertainty. This principle states that in trying to measure two parameters of a particle — for instance, its momentum and its position — we find that the more accurately we can measure its momentum, the less we can know about its position, and vice versa. (Momentum simply means: mass x velocity.)

If we want to measure either the momentum or the position of a particle, we can measure precisely only one of these quantities. If we know the exact momentum of a particle, then its position is completely indefinite or unknowable, and vice versa. This is an example of those strange ways in which particles of atomic size or smaller behave.

We know that at rest, when the pendulum is changing direction, its velocity is zero. But the momentum, at low speeds at least, is equal to *velocity* multiplied by *mass*. However, if we multiply any quantity by a zero, we get zero. Thus, we have now established that the momentum of the pendulum at that point is zero, that is, we know its value very precisely: *It's zero.* But we have said before that if we know precisely the momentum of a particle, then its position becomes diffuse and completely indefinite. That is, the pendulum can be just about any place, even at the end of the universe. Yes, but it has very little time to get there because this whole event occurs in zero time. So there we go again. The pendulum has to disappear in all directions at infinite velocity. It will have to expand very rapidly into space, like a balloon, and then collapse just as rapidly.

Having done this, it comes back, picks up speed, and goes about its usual good-natured business as if nothing had happened. None of us would suspect the leisurely pendulum of doing such a wild thing when no one is looking! But then again, one cannot rely on appearances.

To bring in a more easily digestible model for this behavior, let us take a camera. Suppose that we want to photograph a bird in flight by prevailing light. We know that if we want to get a sharp picture of the bird, we have to use a very short exposure time, say, .001 second. We look at our exposure meter and we find that at .001 second we won't have enough light to register the image on the film, and to get sufficient light we would need at least a .1 second exposure. But we know that in .1 second the bird will be out of sight, and all we shall see on the picture would be a streak representing the bird. So we are in trouble either way. In other words, you can't have your cake and eat it, too.

We have so far been using the pendulum as an example. But a pendulum represents any system that oscillates or moves back and forth, whether such an oscillator pulsates concentrically, goes around in orbits, or turns about itself. From the standpoint of one observer, there are always two points at which either of these systems appears to be at rest. But to be completely at rest — that is, being at the point at which movement in one direction is changing sign or reversing direction — that point of rest implies somehow a disappearance of matter and a movement at infinite or almost infinite velocities. Infinite speed and total rest seem somehow complementary.

Until now we used the pendulum as a model because it is easy to visualize. However, the atoms of matter at room temperature vibrate at a rate of about 10^{15} Hz.; therefore, it is very likely that our matter is blinking off and on at that rate.

Objective and subjective realities

In Chapter 2 we looked through a supermicroscope and discovered that our *objective reality* is made up of void,

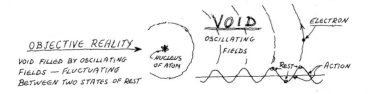

vacuum, which is filled by pulsating, oscillating electro-magnetic fields that in turn move between two points of rest. Each of the points of rest is reached through a period of motion.

In the beginning of this chapter we tried to analyze the nature of our subjective reality. We know that it consists of the sum total of impressions conveyed to us by our senses. Then we found that our nervous systems translate the objective reality for us in a Morse code of action or motion and rest, which are oscillating electrical states of the nervous system.

We can thus extract a common denominator of our objective and subjective realities. We shall find that both realities become *"real" only due to the change or motion occurring between the two states of rest.* In other words, if there is no change, we have a state of perpetual rest, and a state of perpetual rest means *no perceptible reality.*

It may be useful for us to ponder the possibility that "tangible reality" exists for us only as long as there is movement; and when the movement stops, matter and solid reality become diffuse and disappear. At this point, I can no longer resist the temptation to quote from a book by Alexandra David-Neel and Luma Yongden* entitled *The Secret Oral Teachings In Tibetan Buddhist Sects:*

---

* David-Neel, Alexandra, and Yongden, Lama. San Francisco: City Light Books, 1967.

The tangible world *is* movement, say the Masters, not a collection of moving objects, but movement itself. There are no objects "in movements," it is the movement which constitutes the objects which appear to us: they are nothing but movement.

This movement is a continued and infinitely rapid succession of flashes of energy (in Tibetan "tsal" or "shoug"). All objects perceptible to our senses, all phenomena of whatever kind and whatever aspect they may assume, are constituted by a rapid succession of instantaneous events.

There are two theories and both consider the world as movement. One states that the course of this movement (which creates phenomena) is continuous, as the flow of a quiet river seems to us. The other declares that the movement is intermittent and advances by separate flashes of energy which follow each other at such small intervals that these intervals are almost non-existent.

It seems that someone was here before. But where does matter go when it periodically disappears? And what happens to us as we blink on and off? We will learn about this in the following chapters.

Summary

Our senses translate to us the physical reality in a Morse code of *action and rest*. This is our *subjective reality*.

We can compare this action-and-rest language to the motion of a pendulum or an oscillator.

We have shown that when the pendulum reaches its point of rest, it has to become nonmaterial for a very short period of time and expand into space at an almost infinite velocity.

A quote from a Tibetan Buddhist book suggests the same: "Tangible world is movement."

Without change or movement there is no objective or subjective reality.

4. AN EXPERIMENT WITH TIME

Before we start this chapter, it would be good to remind the reader of the purpose of this book, as described in the Introduction. We are faced here with phenomena that are difficult to explain. It will take many years before science will have even a rudimentary understanding of mental phenomena. It is common practice in science to try to make a "model," which describes a certain set of phenomena closely. It may be a rudimentary model at first, which will be refined later as more knowledge of the area becomes available. A successful model for any set of phenomena has to fit these phenomena in a simple and economical way. The more new tenets are required to build the model, the more cumbersome and more vulnerable it becomes.

Rick H.

Knowledge moves in an ever-expanding upward spiral, which allows us to see from the higher turns of the spiral our previous knowledge in a broader perspective. Thus, Newton's mechanics have become a "special case" within Einstein's theory of relativity. So, eventually, will Einstein's theory of relativity become a "special case" in a science that will account for both physical and mental phenomena.

New and more sensitive methods and instruments enable us to do increasingly sophisticated measurements. We can now measure magnetic fields around our heads due to the tiny electric currents in the brain. We can make highly sophisticated measurements that show that whenever there is the slightest change in any system in the body, all other systems are somehow affected. No longer can we view our body as a collection of separate organs thrown into a bag in which a specialist can fix one organ without affecting the others.

As is the body, so is the society and the whole planet, the solar system, and, indeed, the whole cosmos. I hope to show, by the time we come to the end of this book, that we are part of a highly integrated system in the broadest sense of the word.

However, back to our model. In it we'll try to tie together as many diverse phenomena as possible and fit them into a compact system. The physical, objective phenomena serve as a starting point for this model.

Experiment with time

In the previous chapters, we talked about the action of the nervous system, which receives input from the environment and codes it for us in an action-rest language. This action is, naturally, occurring in *time*, that is, it takes time for any of these events to happen.

When we think of time, we think of clock time. Action all around the world is synchronized by clock time, starting with train schedules, worldwide plane schedules, navigation, astronomy, worldwide telecommunication, etc. These depend completely on accurate timing. The accuracy standards of timekeeping devices have been increasing rapidly due to the demands for more and more accurate timing for space communication, navigation, astronomy, etc. Rather than use mechanical clocks, we are relying nowadays on "atomic clocks." This is not a clock in the usual sense but a device that uses the very stable oscillation of the cesium atoms as a standard for timekeeping.

From grandfather clocks to wrist watches, all these clocks are supposed to chop up for us the 24 hours of the day more or less reliably into hours, minutes, and seconds. Let's call this kind of time "objective" since everybody's watches are supposed to cut time into slices of even thickness. However, we know from personal experience that time does not "feel" as passing evenly under different circumstances. When pursuing some interesting activity, time "flies"; while waiting in the dentist's office, it "drags." When Einstein was once asked about this "psychological time," he replied with a now famous observation: "When you spend two hours with a nice girl, you think it's only a minute. But when you sit on a hot stove for a minute, you think it's two hours." Having thus "firmly" established the relativity of time, let us see, then, how this subjective time can be put to some use.

We know from sleep studies that during dreaming periods time dilation occurs. In other words, if, for example, a person is awakened after a very brief period of active dreaming and is asked to describe what happened in his dream, usually a long story will come out, which would have taken a much longer period of objective time to occur.

We also know that under hypnosis time dilation can take place* and can easily be noticed. Studies on such mind-affecting drugs as cannabis, LSD, etc., indicate that time distortions occur. Since these materials are not unknown substances to most readers of this book, we may possibly use

* Le Cron, Leslie M. *Experimental Hypnosis*. New York: Macmillan, 1952, p. 217.

them as an example. When listening to someone talk while under the influence of some of the mind-affecting drugs, the feeling is that the speaker is talking very slowly and that the pauses between words are extremely long. In fact, we are sure that that we could easily run once around the block before the next word comes out. There is no change in the pitch of the sound of the words, that is, the words do not sound like tape-recorded speech on slow speed. Clearly, what happens is that we somehow have more subjective time, and we can observe the act of speech in greater detail. Have our mental processes been speeded up relative to those of the speaker? Or do we simply have more time in which to observe the event?

Let's try an experiment that should shed light on this dilemma. When a person has been trained by biofeedback to produce theta waves or can put himself into a deep meditative state and at the same time is able to watch the second hand of a clock in front of him, he will be surprised to find that the second hand has come to a stop. It's a rather startling experience, and the natural reaction to it is: "This is impossible!"* At that moment, the second hand will accelerate and resume its normal rate. However, if we can get over this reaction and watch with half-open eyes the face of the clock, while all the time being in a deep meditative state, then we can keep the second hand from moving for as long as we wish.

The above experiment is naturally limited to people who have especially good control over their states of consciousness. I have designed an experiment that is within easy reach of practically anybody who wants to experience this change in time, at least in a minor way. It does not require any training or any drugs. The only thing we need is a clock with a second hand or a wrist watch with a fairly large dial and an easily visible second hand.

Step 1. Relax. Position the watch in front of you on a table so that it will be easily visible without any effort through half-closed eyes. Lean with your elbows on the table if you wish.

* Floyd, Keith. "Of Time and Mind." In White, John, ed.: *Frontiers of Consciousness*. New York: Julian Press, 1974.

Step 2. Look at the watch in a relaxed way and follow the second hand. Try to absorb and remember the rhythm at which it moves. All this has to be done quite effortlessly.

Step 3. This is the crucial step in the experiment. Close your eyes and visualize yourself engaged in your most favorite activity. This visualization has to be as perfect as possible. For instance, if you visualize yourself lying on a beach in the sun, you have to *be there* — all of you. Don't just *think* you are there, but feel the warmth of the sun and the texture of the sand; hear the sound of the waves; use all your senses. The results will be better if you choose a relaxing activity rather than a hectic one.

4. When you feel that you have stabilized this visualization, slowly open your eyes just a bit. *Don't focus on the watch,* just let your gaze fall on the dial as if you are a disinterested observer of this whole affair. If you have followed the instructions properly, you may see the second hand stick in a few places, slow down, and hover for a while. If you are very successful, you'll be able to stop the second hand for quite a while.

To some people this is a shocking experience. The moment one feels shocked, the second hand accelerates and resumes its normal speed. Clearly, there is something very disturbing here.

We have described several instances in which time is being somehow manipulated. I'm not saying that we have actually slowed down the movement of the clock. It is still keeping good old objective time. But we did stretch our subjective time so that we are facing a *subjective* situation that in turn provides an analogy to a well-known objective situation. This was first made clear in the theory of relativity, in which it was shown that two observers moving relative to each other do not agree on the rates at which their respective clocks are running.

Let us try to analyze what is common to all the cases. We find that the connecting link is an altered state of consciousness.* Some may claim that the last experiment has nothing to do with altered states of consciousness; in fact, some will

* Tart, Charles T. *Altered States of Consciousness.* New York: Wiley, 1969, pp. 335-45; London: Wiley, 1969.

altogether deny the existence of such a thing as consciousness.

Why, then, did the watch slow down or stop altogether for
a while? I propose that the observing mind (or "the observer," for short), the entity that correlates and makes sense of
the information submitted to it by the brain, was absent. It
went off to the beach and left the "hardware" at home, unat-
tended. The "hardware," by which I mean the sensory
organs and the brain, are processing and producing the
information, but the. *entity* that correlates and makes sense
of the information, has left the body for a while.

This is not as frivolous as it may sound.* Such a hypothetical AWOL "observer" could have been noticed on the
beach by a so-called "sensitive" or clairvoyant person under
the right conditions. While the "observer" was busy correlat-
ing the information coming to him from the beach, he
could not handle the information presented to him by the
physical eyes gazing at the watch.

From the moment the watch stopped to the moment it
started moving again, the "observer" was "out of the body."
In cases in which the watch has only slowed down, the
"observer" was "split." He was partially on the beach and

* Monroe, Robert A. *Journeys Out of the Body*. New York:
Doubleday & Co., 1971; London: Souvenir Press, 1972. Targ, Rus-
sell and Puthoff, Harold. "Remote Viewing of Natural Targets,"
Parapsychol. Rev. 6: 1975, pp. 1-3.

partially in the body, handling information at a reduced rate. In the following chapters, I intend to discuss how all these strange doings of the "observer" can take place. For the time being we shall stay with the results of our experiment and try to make sense of them.

In the case of the complete stopping of the watch, the eyes have become an inert camera, projecting to the screen of the brain the last information they have seen before the departure of the "observer." This is analogous to the little mini-calculators in use today. The screen displays and holds the last information the operator has punched in.

An alert reader has probably noticed by now an interesting property of this "observer": He can flit about to distant places in fractions of a second. He may leave his physical body and be off to a beach thousands of miles away and be back all within one or two seconds.

In the previous chapter we discussed the behavior of oscillators and pendulums. Let's recall what happens when a pendulum comes to one of its extreme positions. We found that between the points at which the pendulum has to come to a full stop and the point at which it started on its return trip, there is an area in which causal relationship between time and space breaks down, in which its position "smears out" and infinite or nearly infinite velocities are encountered because of the uncertainty principle operating on the quantum scale of things.

We know that we cannot accelerate physical objects to the velocity of light, not to speak of infinite velocities. But under the conditions we are discussing, physical matter loses its definiteness, it becomes less "solid" thus making it easier for the observer to separate from it. Our bodies, as we know from Chapter 1, behave in pendulum-like fashion. It is possible that the "observer," having no physical mass, could be flitting back and forth at very high velocities with each up and down movement of the body? And if this is the case, where does it go?

A simple diagram will help us to put in order the previously discussed phenomena. (Do not be intimidated by diagrams. The author has full understanding of most people's distaste for mathematics, graphs, etc. However, diagrams

communicate better and faster than words. So just bear with
it for a while; it will be over quickly.) In Figure 23 our four-
dimensional space-time is represented by two lines: the vertical direction stands for time, the horizontal direction represents space. Let us remember that space has three
dimensions, but here they are represented by the horizontal
directions only. Passage of time into the future is shown as
movement upward, above the horizontal line, while all that
happened in the past is shown below it. The crossing point
of the horizontal and the vertical lines represents our
"now." It is the starting point for any event.

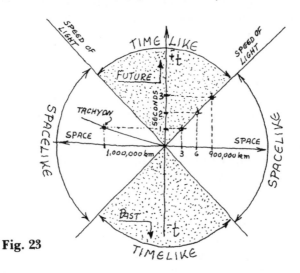

Fig. 23

Let us try to make use of this diagram and see how a
photon, which is a particle of light, would behave on this
diagram. We know that light travels at about 300,000
kilometer/second. So, starting from the "now" point, we
mark off on the vertical line our units of time: 1, 2, 3 seconds.
On the horizontal line we mark off the distance traveled by
that particle: For the first second it has traveled 300,000
kilometers, for the next second 600,000 kilometers, for the
third second 900,000 kilometers.

From the points on the vertical line, which indicate time
units, we shall now extend dotted horizontal lines, and from

the points on the horizontal line, which indicate units of distance, we shall extend dotted vertical lines. These lines will cross, and through their points of intersection we shall draw a diagonal line, starting from the "now" point. We can extend this diagonal line below the "now" point into the past, and we can draw a symmetrical diagonal line, also going through the "now" point down into the past. These two diagonals will outline two triangles touching the "now" with their tips. Their bases are open, of course, because we cannot put any limits on the past or the future. In fact, we can visualize the point of "now" as moving into the future, leaving in its wake many "nows" which make up our past. We can also say that the upper (shaded) triangle describes the activities that will occur in the future, while the bottom shaded triangle represents the events of the past.

The fastest action in the physical world is naturally limited by the speed of light. Therefore, the diagonal lines representing the speed of light set the limits to the speed at which an object can travel within our physical universe. Physicists call this behavior "timelike," referring to our normal space-time universe, because all action on this diagram which occurs below the speed of light will tend to cluster around the vertical time axis.

In spite of all these apparent limitations, there are courageous physicists who are working on hypothetical particles, called *tachyons*, which can move at speeds higher than light. The speed of tachyons starts just above the speed of light and it ranges all the way to infinite velocities.*

This brings us to the other portion of our diagram. Suppose that we have a tachyon going at an almost infinite speed, which implies that it is moving practically along the horizontal space axis only. It is going so fast that it uses up almost no time. In the previous example it took the photon three seconds to traverse the 900,000 kilometers, as shown in the diagram. The tachyon will travel that distance in practically no time at all, so that we can plot its movement on the horizontal without regard to the vertical time axis. There is

* Bilaniuk, Olexa-Myron and Sudarshan, E. C. *Physics Today*, May 1969, Vol. 22.

nothing to be marked off on the vertical scale, since almost no time was used for the motion of this tachyon.

Suppose now that the tachyon slows down at one million kilometers/second. This is still considerably faster than the speed of light, and the point representing the speed of the tachyon will naturally be marked off on the vertical line, as shown in the diagram. However, it will appear closer to the horizontal than to the vertical axis. In short, all speeds that are faster than the speed of light will tend to cluster around the horizontal space axis, and therefore such behavior is called by the physicists "space-like." Speeds at which space is traversed while very little time is used up will be termed "spacelike" activity.

When something moves so fast that it uses almost no time for its movement then it moves at an *almost infinite speed,* and when something is going so fast, then it must be present at all places at once! We mortals could perhaps give this kind of behavior a more fitting name: *omnipresence.* This is a very important concept on which we shall expand later.

Omnipresence

We have all heard about the supersonic planes crossing the Atlantic in an hour and a half. Our astronauts are crossing the Atlantic in about 15 minutes. Suppose now that a plane were developed that could shuttle back and forth between London and New York in half a minute. Imagine yourself asking the stewardess on such a plane as to your whereabouts. She will say: "We have momentarily left New York — we are approaching London — oops! We are on our way back to New York." Clearly, our question makes no sense. We may just have to accept the fact that we are somehow in both places more or less at once.

Now suppose that we build a vehicle that can travel almost as fast as light. This means that we could go around our planet about seven times per second. This allows us to see practically any point on our globe within a second. And the people on the earth may see us always at one point or another, so that we are forming a shell of "presence" around the earth.

Let's now visualize that we move at almost infinite speeds. Then it's easy to see that we can go around and through our solar system (or galaxy, or universe, for that matter) many times a second, thus weaving a tight pattern throughout that system. We could see everything there is to see and be everywhere in practically no time at all. In other words, we would have become *omnipresent*.

After the novelty of being omnipresent has worn off, and we have become accustomed to the high speeds, we feel that it is insufficient just to whiz around so fast. We would also like to know what goes on in our solar system. For that we have to invent a very rapid information-processing computer, which we can build cheaply and quickly in our imagination. We can absorb all the information about the solar system as it comes in. We are now not only omnipresent but omniscient.

We find ourselves spread throughout and around the solar system in a shimmering, vibrating shell, all-seeing and all knowing. After all the difficulties in attaining this great technical feat are forgotten, the attainment of almost infinite speeds becomes commonplace to us. Now we turn inside and begin to contemplate our state, and we arrive at the paradoxical conclusion that going so fast is really the same as *being at rest*, in all places at once! We come to the conclusion that if we could only expand our consciousness, somehow, our "observer-mind" could fill all space and would not need to run so fast. Also, we now understand that attaining infinite speed would mean attaining another, higher state of rest or *state of being*. The circle closes here.

It is time now to go back to our diagrams.

Let's make a diagram similar to Figure 23, with the same "objective" coordinates. By "objective coordinates" we mean that they represent space and time as we normally know them. But parallel to these objective coordinates let's add broken lines representing our subjective coordinates in subjective space and subjective time (Fig. 24). In our "normal" waking state of consciousness, these two coordinate systems stay parallel and overlap. Most of the time, however, there is a periodic fluctuation, which repeats approximately every 1½ hours.*

Fig. 24

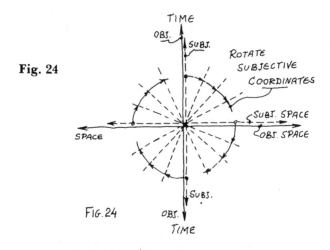

FIG. 24

I suggest that during altered states of consciousness our subjective time-space coordinates separate from the objective coordinates and rotate about the common center, as shown in Figure 25. Let's rotate the subjective coordinates by an arbitrary angle, which we'll call ‡ (psi), and draw a line parallel to the horizontal objective space axis through the 1-second mark. (This represents the projection of one objective second onto our subjective time.) Now let us find on it the intersection with the subjective time, t_{subj}. By measuring the length of the diagonal line from the "now" to the intersection, we find that our subjective time unit is longer than the objective one. In short, it looks as if we have *more time* than before to do what we are engaged in doing. In fact, for the angle chosen in the diagram, we have at our disposal four subjective seconds to one objective second.

* Lavie, Peretz and Kripke, Daniel F. *Psychology Today*, April 1975, p. 54.

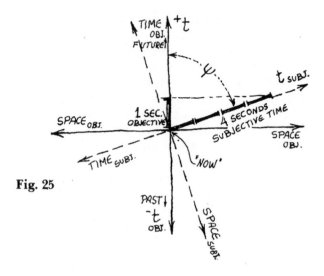

Fig. 25

Let us return to the person under the influence of a mind-affecting drug who is listening to someone speak. Suppose that the speaker utters one word per second. The person under the influence of the drug and presumably in an altered state of consciousness will have more subjective time to listen to the word and will therefore be in a better position to analyze the word because his mental processes are operating at the normal objective rate.

A simple example will provide an analogy for this phenomenon. Suppose that we take a pole with knots on it. When the sun is at a low angle, the shadow of the pole becomes very long, so that we can examine the knots and the spaces between them in more detail (Fig. 26).

Fig. 26

The alert reader will probably remark here: "Why complicate things so much? Most of these phenomena can be accounted for simply by assuming that our mental processes have speeded up considerably, and that therefore the sharpness of our perception has been greatly increased. We don't need subjective time and space to explain time distortions."

This, however, is not quite the case, as we shall see later. Looking back at the diagram, we come to realize that any additional increase in ‡ angle will increase subjective time enormously.* As our subjective time axis leans closer to the horizontal, we find that we may have maybe a million subjective seconds to every objective second, because the point of intersection between the horizontal line, marking the one second point of objective time, will meet our tilted subjective time axis very far from the "now" point. And when our subjective time axis becomes finally horizontal, our subjective time becomes infinitely long, so that under these conditions we are using no objective time at all.†

At this point it would be useful to sum up what we have learned from the two space-time diagrams. From Figure 23 we know that the faster something moves, the closer it comes to the horizontal line, i.e., it exhibits a "spacelike" behavior. From Figure 25 we see that the more our "subjective time" axis leans to the horizontal, the more subjective time we have on hand. If we combine these two diagrams, we have to conclude that a tilting of our subjective time axis causes us to behave in an increasingly "spacelike" manner, which means that in an altered state of consciousness we are rapidly expanding into space. In other words, *an expansion of consciousness leads to an expansion into space.* This may occur at speeds below or above that of light.

* The values for the $\frac{t \text{ subj.}}{t \text{ obj.}}$ ratio go up rapidly as we go beyond 89 degrees. At 89.9 degrees this ratio is about 573. It goes beyond one million above 89.9999 degrees.

† When the angle ‡ becomes 90 degrees, then the subjective time becomes infinitely long. This is because the cosine of 90 degrees is zero. Hence:

Subjective time = $\dfrac{1}{\cos ‡}$ = $\dfrac{1}{0}$ = ∞ = infinity.

Here the attentive reader has probably noticed that in our subjective time we have unceremoniously slipped through the velocity of light barrier. This is something that no physical object can do; but our "observer," being a nonphysical entity, will have no problems doing this. However, the "observer" is still tenuously linked to the physical body, and the physical senses still relay messages to him in an undistorted form. He still operates, although loosely, against a background of physical spacetime. By crossing the speed-of-light barrier, he finds himself in a spacelike universe. This is a strange new universe in which there is no limit on speed, in which time is being converted into space.

The "off and on" us

It is time now for us to start putting together the assumed bizarre behavior of the pendulum or oscillator discussed in Chapter 3. When the distances per unit time at the extreme point, through which the pendulum is moving, become extremely small, almost infinite or infinite speeds are encountered. But infinite speeds of what? The answer seems to be: infinite speed of a nonphysical entity, the "observer," while the physical body loses its definiteness in space. (We cannot know its position.) The "observer" retains its integrity as an information-processing unit in spite of its rapid expansion into space, while all we can say about the physical body is that it "blinks" off and on twice per each oscillation, at the points of rest.

So as our bodies oscillate up and down about seven times a second, the "observer" expands at the end of each movement for an extremely short period of objective time, then contracts, unaware of the event. In other words, our $\ddagger$ angle momentarily opens up and closes again, back and parallel with objective time. This would happen about fourteen times a second since we have two points of rest per cycle. Normally, we retain no memory of the event. However, the "observer" can cover long distances within this very short period of time and observe many things. No wonder then, that he can be off to a distant beach and be back in a few seconds.

As our ability to hold an expanded state of consciousness increases, the ‡ angle does not close and become zero but fluctuates at some distance from the objective time axis. This increases our subjective time, so that we can start remembering some information we have received while out of the body.

From all the above it follows that we may describe a person's level of consciousness *by the ratio of his subjective time to his objective time.* The range of these ratios is very broad. It starts with small differences, which normally would be taken for just a "wandering of attention" (our little experiment with the clock), to hypnotic time dilation, to dreaming, which is clearly an altered state of consciousness. And, finally, to a deep meditative state, in which time is "stopped" or almost "stopped." We can express this in a simple mathematical form:

level of consciousness index = $\dfrac{\text{subjective time}}{\text{objective time}}$. Or take

our example from Figure 25: $\dfrac{\text{subjective time} = 4 \text{ seconds}}{\text{objective time} = 1 \text{ second}}$

$= \dfrac{4}{1} = 4$. This is our "level of consciousness index."

We have not up to this point focused on what is happening to our subjective space coordinate, which rotates together with the subjective time coordinate. As the subjective time stretches, so does the "observer" expand into his subjective space. (Remember, the space coordinate represents three-dimensional space.)

After "tunneling" from our timelike to the spacelike dimension, our space axis approaches the objective time axis. This carries with it some startling consequences. Our timelike subjective space is becoming objective time. This means that our "observer," as he travels in what he considers his space, is actually *moving through his own and other people's objective time* either into the past or into the future. This may perhaps explain the mechanism by which clairvoyants* operate. They seem to be able to describe the past, some of them surprisingly well. They may even possibly predict the future, but since the future is made up of probabilities dependent on human free will, such travel into the future would be rather vague and unreliable (Fig. 27).

When one asks a clairvoyant how he "does his thing," he answers: "I'm going into your past." He has a feeling of moving through time. Time is space for him.

Let us return to our experiment with the clock. I have asked you to visualize a favorite activity. This automatically programmed your "observer" to move into the past because your favorite activity can only be an experience of the past. Your "observer" moved into the past and was off to a beach in a wink and back in another wink; he went in his subjective time and space into a different "reality." One can consider projecting one's "observer" into the future, if this is not too strenuous. Again, time will slow down.

All this sounds very confusing at first. However, it's a rather simple and compact way of explaining many puzzling phenomena to which there are as yet no scientific explanations.

What, then, does reality consist of? How do we see reality in the light of all this?

EXCHANGING OBJECTIVE TIME FOR SUBJECTIVE SPACE...

Fig. 27

Rick

* Clairvoyants are people who can operate without the constraints of space and time and can see and describe events occurring in the past and the future, both in the physical and the nonphysical realms.

Our Solid and Not So Solid Realities

Let's go back to the pendulum, which is our body. It oscillates up and down about seven times a second. Each time the body comes to a rest (fourteen times a second) the "observer" expands at a very high speed through his subjective time into objective space. This expansion takes practically no time. Figure 28 describes the relationship between our different realities. Our solid physical reality goes on, as usual, except for tiny pauses, during which our "observer" takes off and comes back. During the "out" periods, in the other dimensions or realities, an untrained "observer" comes back without communicating any knowledge of this outing to the mind and the brain. In other words, this experience does not normally reach the conscious thinking level.

A very good example of this is so-called "subliminal advertising." This was a technique used some years ago by which products were advertised in the movie theaters or on television by flashing for a very short time a message on the screen. The public was never aware of what was happening since the message was too short to activate the conscious mind into producing a coherent thought image. But the subconscious mind, being much quicker, did pick up the message, and people dutifully consumed the advertised products. These techniques have fortunately since been outlawed.

A trained "observer" (the one who can stay at a high level of consciousness for a while) has, as shown before, managed to stretch his subjective time considerably. Naturally, he may be able to observe and be imprinted with the information he sees. Then, upon his return, he may formulate the imprinted visions into thoughts.

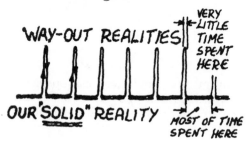

Fig. 28

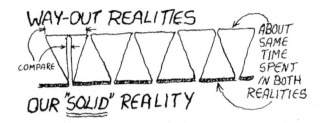

Fig. 29

While one is in an expanded state of consciousness, his reality diagram differs from that of Figure 28 and looks rather like Figure 29. If you notice the top line, his other reality has become as continuous and stretched out as his physical reality. He is spending as much time there as on the physical level (not in actual objective time). He should, therefore, be able to make a coherent picture of his experiences and describe what he sees there. The development of the ability to retain the information will be explained in the coming chapters.

We have until now used the 7 Hz. rate of motion of the body as a trigger for the "ejection" of the observer. But as you may remember from Chapter 3, any oscillator will tend to disappear and reappear at its own rate. The atoms of our bodies are such oscillators; they vibrate at a rate of about 10^{15} Hz. It is possible that our bodies blink on and off at this very high rate. There is no way of knowing whether this is so since presently we have no way of registering such rapid phenomena. However, we cannot assume that all the atoms in our bodies beat synchronously or coherently. We have to visualize our bodies blinking on and off gradually, different areas disappearing, others appearing. In other words, we are partially "out" all the time. This does not, however, alter the basic model presented here since it does not matter how long the on and off periods are.

In the unlikely event that total coherency occurs in the body (this may occur at very high levels of consciousness), then, naturally, the whole body will blink off and on as a unit, and we may expect to see some very unusual things occurring in such a state. We took the 7 Hz. pulsation as the minimum number of on and off periods since that is a measurable figure.

Summary

An experiment with time shows that we have objective and subjective space-time, which normally coincide.

Under altered states of consciousness, these two become separated, and we can function in our subjective space-time.

This explains many phenomena, such as clairvoyance, telepathy, etc.

We postulate an "observer," which is our "psyche," and which becomes "omnipresent" for a very short period of time. This is the time required for the pendulum or oscillator to change its direction of motion.

Our bodies are oscillators, and the atoms making up our bodies are also oscillators. Therefore, we expand into a spacelike dimension many times a second very rapidly and collapse back as rapidly, possibly at the rate of atomic vibration. However, *in an altered state of consciousness we can expand our subjective time greatly.* This allows us to observe the action of other psyches that are "out there" at a leisurely pace and bring back useful information from "there." This is done without using up much objective time.

So our reality is made up of a constant rapid back-and-forth shuttling between our solid reality and the way-out realities, which we share with everybody else.

An expanded or higher state of consciousness implies an expansion of our psyche into space.

5. QUANTITY AND QUALITY OF CONSCIOUSNESS

In the previous chapter, we talked about altered states of consciousness and even managed to define levels of consciousness as being somehow connected with the ratio of subjective to objective time. We must now attempt to interpret what the "level of consciousness" means and how it fits into the scheme of things.

Let us first try to define "consciousness" in the simplest possible terms. We can say that it is the capacity of a system to respond to stimuli. This system may also be a nervous system, no matter how simple. Suppose we stimulate an atom by applying ultraviolet light or other electromagnetic radiation to it. One or more of the electrons may get excited and respond by jumping into a higher orbit farther away from the nucleus. When we remove this stimulus, these electrons may drop back into their previous orbits and emit photons of a certain energy or frequency in the process. By applying different stimuli, we shall elicit different responses from this system.

Next let us take a virus and stimulate it. It will react with a number of different responses. If we take a bacterium and tickle it, it will react with an even larger number of responses than the virus: it may giggle or wriggle its flagellae, etc. The higher and the more complex the organism, the more varied and the more numerous the responses per stimulus. When we come to mammals and eventually humans, the number of possible responses grows rapidly. So let us define this number as the *quantity of consciousness*. This admittedly sounds quite arbitrary, but let us proceed first on the assumption that the number of responses of a system can be equated with "consciousness." We may at first have trouble trying to visualize a rock or an atom as a living thing because we associate consciousness with life. But this notion is just a human limitation; a rock may also have difficulty in understanding human consciousness. At present we restrict the term "live beings" to beings that can reproduce. This, I believe, is quite arbitrary. We seem to project our own behavior onto other systems, by saying that starting from the atom and going to larger aggregates there is no "life," and then suddenly, when the aggregates of atoms have reached a certain stage of organization, "life" appears, because we can recognize our own behavior in it. My basic premise is that consciousness resides in matter; put another way, all mass (matter) contains consciousness (or life) to a greater or lesser extent. It may be refined or primitive. We human beings are so designed that when properly trained, we can interact with anything that has consciousness on whatever level.

We have said that the atom has consciousness because it can respond to stimuli. Now all physical reality is constructed of atoms in smaller or larger aggregates. Consequently, we can say that a given mass contains such and such a percentage of consciousness. This percentage will vary in quantity and in quality according to the different evolutionary levels.

There is a certain relationship between the number of responses per stimulus, or *quantity of consciousness*, and the level of consciousness, or the *quality of consciousness*. We shall express the quality of consciousness in terms of frequency response. The higher the quality of consciousness, the higher the frequency-response range of the system. We know that our ears respond to stimuli (sound) ranging from about 30 Hz to 20,000 Hz. So we can say that our hearing mechanism has a frequency response of 30 to 20,000 Hz. We know that our vision has also a limited frequency response, and so do all our senses.

Thus, the "quality of consciousness" defines the degree of refinement of such a response and its range. We could also equate it with the intelligence of the response. It is important to note that the quantity of consciousness has nothing to do with the size or bulk of the entity. It stands only for the number of responses it is capable of.

We shall make a diagram now to show the relationship of these two aspects of consciousness. See Figure 30. On the horizontal line we plot the quantity of consciousness; and on the vertical line, its quality. Let us use the atom as a basic unit of consciousness and assign an arbitrary scale of numbers to the various categories of beings. We shall designate the frequency response of the atom as f_1; next would come a virus, f_2; a plant, f_3; a dog, f_4; and finally, a human, f_5. We shall place the highly developed intelligent human beings at f_6. The band between f_5 and f_6 represents the responses of the human nervous system to all the possible stimuli delivered to it by our senses. This includes instruments that we use as extensions of our senses.

Let me make this clearer. Suppose that we take a picture of a woman sitting at a table. We show it to a man of limited perception and ask him to describe what he is seeing. The

QUANTITY AND QUALITY OF CONSCIOUSNESS

THE ABSOLUTE

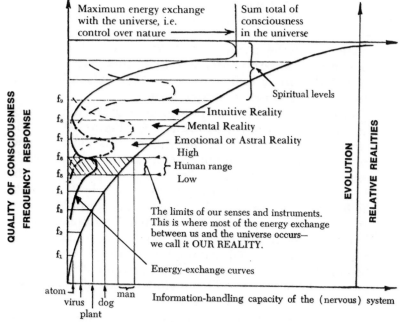

Fig. 30   **QUANTITY OF CONSCIOUSNESS**

QUANTITY OF CONSCIOUSNESS:
Given in terms of the number of responses a system is capable of as a reaction to a stimulus.

QUALITY OF CONSCIOUSNESS:
The degree of *refinement* or intelligence of such responses and their range, expressed in terms of frequency response. Each frequency range stands for a certain reality band.

RELATIVE REALITIES:
All reality bands below the ABSOLUTE.

ABSOLUTE:
The sum total of consciousness in the universe.

ENERGY-EXCHANGE CURVES:
These curves show the extent of energy exchange between an entity and its environment. Thus, maximum energy exchange, or interactions of human beings with their environment, occurs at the peak of the curve. It is our point of resonance with the environment.

probable answer will be "a woman sitting at a table." Let us show the same picture to another person. He will describe in great detail the style, the composition, the color scheme, etc. We shall probably have to stop him from talking too much. This man has a broader range and refinement of responses and therefore will describe the picture with greater fidelity.

Thus, the band width f_5 to f_6 expresses the responses of the human nervous system to all possible stimuli. Our physical reality is conveyed to us by all the possible inputs to our sensory system. This system codes the information in an action-and-rest code, as we have described in Chapter 3, from which our brain constructs our reality. But then the other bands in this diagram, the ones above the human frequency-response band (such as f_7 and f_8 or the ones below it), must also represent the realities for the population occupying those levels. In short, what we are dealing with here are actually different realities, higher and lower than our own in terms of the evolution of matter in the universe.

Out of this it appears that in Nature we have a spectrum of realities, each occupied by a population having a certain level of consciousness. What may sound unusual is that I am suggesting that a mineral or a vegetable also has some consciousness and forms a reality of its own. I hope to convince you of the validity of this point of view as we go along. This spectrum of realities should not be looked at as having sharply defined boundaries, but rather is similar to the electromagnetic radiation band we call the visual spectrum, which contains radiation between about 4,000 to 8,000 angstroms in wavelength (1 angstrom = 10^{-10} meter). We say that it contains colors ranging from violet to deep red, going through blue, green, yellow, etc. There are no sharp defining lines between the colors that separate them; they blend into each other smoothly.

Let us now look at the diagram as a whole. We see that the relationship between the quantity and the quality of consciousness is given by a curved line. We note that the curved line becomes almost parallel with the horizontal line at the top which we shall call the "absolute." Note that for each jump from one reality to the next higher one, say from f_2 to f_3, there is a relatively small increase in the quantity of consciousness; while in the higher realities, say, from f_{10} to f_{11}, the increase of the quantity of consciousness is very large. In fact, this increase becomes almost infinitely large as the curve approaches the absolute. We can say, therefore, that the "absolute" contains all consciousness there is in the universe. *It is the source of all consciousness.*

Notice the arrow of evolution, on the right side of the diagram. It points up toward the absolute. This implies that all matter in the universe, starting from the atom, is moving up in levels of consciousness under the forces of evolution until it finally reaches the absolute. It also means that matter is combining and becoming more and more complex, forming more intricate nervous systems as time goes by, and these nervous systems are capable of interacting with nature in more complex patterns. In other words, the quality of their consciousness is increasing.

We now turn to the little bell-shaped curves on the left vertical line. Let us call them "energy-exchange curves." We see that the lower curves close to the bottom line are smaller,

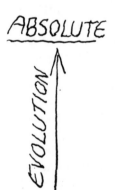

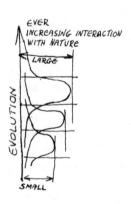

while the higher we go vertically, the more the energy-exchange curves grow in height. As we progress along our evolutionary ladder, our interaction with our environment increases. At the highest levels, this means control over the environment or Nature.

One may ask: How does our reality differ from other realities? The answer is that our nervous system, which interprets reality for us, interacts strongly within the band of frequencies from f_5 to f_6. We are, so to speak, tuned to exchange maximum energy with our present environment and are in resonance with it. This is the meaning of the energy-exchange curve. The peak of the curve lies in the middle of our reality band, but you may note that the curve extends into the next higher reality and the ones below ours, the animal and the plant realities. That is our normal span of interactions; knowingly or unknowingly, we interact with other levels.

We know, for example, that if we try to push our index finger through a table top, we encounter difficulties due to the resistance offered by the table top, or if we drive a car at 60 mph, and it hits a bridge abutment, we do find that there is a strong interaction between us and the abutment. However, if we *dream* that we are driving the same car at 60 mph and hit a bridge abutment, the interaction is not as strong as it would be in our physical reality. We would wake up slightly shaken and say to ourselves: "I'm so glad it was only a dream." This interaction is clearly less strong — and less expensive.

SPIRITUAL

EMOTIONAL

HUMAN

ANIMAL

PLANT

MINERAL

You are probably suspecting by now that somewhere above us there is a reality that is the dream reality. Our energy-exchange curve reaches into and beyond it. The energy-exchange curve of the next level, which we may call (using the existing esoteric terminology) the "astral" level, is higher than ours. The astral curve reaches down into our reality and below it, all the way to the mineral reality. Clearly, the population of the astral reality can affect our reality quite substantially. The important thing to notice is that the peak of their energy-exchange curve is higher than ours, which means that they can interact with their environment and with Nature in general more strongly than we can. They can make things go "bump in the night." Notice also that on the level above the astral, f_8, the energy-exchange curve is still higher — so that their interaction with Nature and therefore the resulting control over Nature is even higher. This level we shall call the "mental" level, as it is called in most literature on esoteric subjects. The level above it will be the "causal" or the intuitive level, which again shows a higher interaction of energies and a larger increase in the quantity of consciousness per reality band.

As we move higher on the scale of evolution, we encounter the so-called spiritual realities. These reach all the way to the absolute. Note the very high energy-exchange curve of the highest, the spiritual level. This implies total control over Nature.

We can sum up the above statements this way: it seems that a continuous spectrum of realities arises due to the ability of matter to contain consciousness. Therefore, a rock will contain less consciousness than a plant or a dog. This entails the rock's lesser degree of control over its environment, fewer possible responses, and therefore less free will (that is, if one can speak about the free will of a rock). But let us not forget that we humans also have only limited free will. The higher we move along the scale of evolution, the higher the degree of free will, and the higher our ability to control or create our own environment.

We also know from Chapter 4 that oscillating or reciprocating systems will tend to go off many times a second with almost infinite speed into the wild blue yonder of the spacelike universe. But since everything and everybody does this (because an atom is an oscillating system), we must all meet and possibly interact during those short periods of time out. In other words, all creation is in constant and instantaneous contact on the level of spacelike universe, with some creatures being more aware of this than others. Therefore, the energy-exchange curve never goes down to zero. There is always some interaction throughout all the levels.

The hierarchy of realities: the absolute

You will remember from previous chapters that our reality is coded in terms of movement and rest. We also remember that when an oscillator is in a state of rest, it tunnels into a spacelike dimension, which implies infinite velocities that are equivalent to a state of rest — it becomes omnipresent. In other words, it has attained a state of just "being" for a very short period of time; but when the oscillator is in a state of movement, business continues as usual. In this way, we have separated these two components of reality: movement and rest.

NoT 0

Now let us look at this state of "being." It is becoming clear that we can equate the state of being with the absolute, since both imply no motion, no action, and total rest. At the same time, though, it is a state of high potential energy, because this state of rest is equivalent to infinitely fast motion. In fact, we may say that the two contrasting concepts of movement and rest become reconciled in the absolute. We can take this state or reality as the baseline, an

absolute reference line against which all else in creation can
be measured. This will then be an ever-present component
in all our realities.

You may remember from our discussion of the hologram
in Chapter 1 that we need two components to form an image
or a "reality." One is the reference frequency beam; the
other, the "experienced" or modulated out-of-phase beam.
Only when these two interact on the same plane do we get
an image. Since this is a device used very extensively by
Nature, we may use it as an analogy here as well. But it is
important to remember that the two beams of the laser light
come from a common source: The single beam is split into
two separate beams. It is the reference beam that has
retained the undisturbed behavior of the source of the light,
while the working beam gets distorted or "modulated" by
its contact with objects it illuminates.

We can use another analogy as an illustration to help
explain the nature of the absolute and the relative aspects of
reality. Let us represent the absolute by the image of a
boundless deep sea. The surface of the sea is very calm and so
smooth as to be invisible (Fig. 31). The absolute is the reference against which we compare everything else. Now let us
ripple the surface of this sea (Fig. 32). We watch the waves
appear and break up the smooth surface. This rippling
makes the surface suddenly visible. By analogy, when
motion or vibration appears in the absolute, it becomes visible or manifest, and we call it the relative, or physical reality.

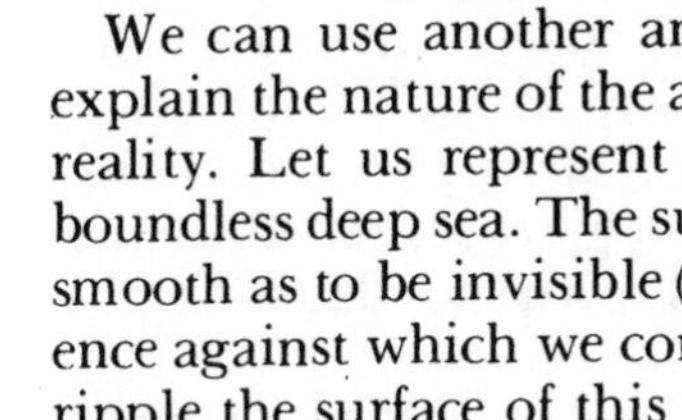

SEA OF THE ABSOLUTE

"BEING" OR
PURE CONSCIOUSNESS

RIPPLES ON THE SURFACE OF THE ABSOLUTE
ARE THE
MANIFEST VISIBLE ASPECT
OF THE ABSOLUTE

Fig. 31 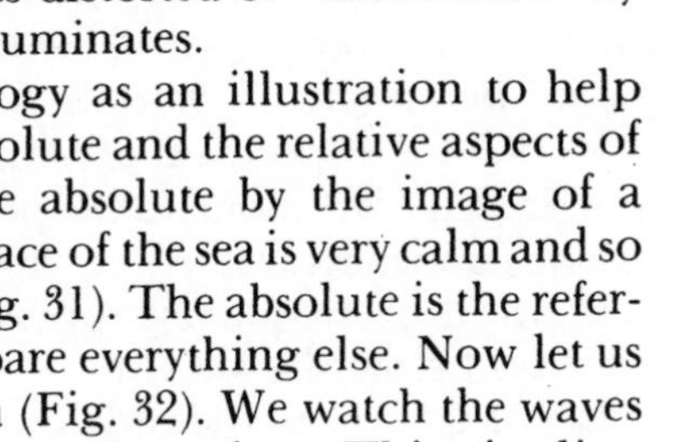   **Fig. 32**

WAVE PACKET

A QUANTUM OF
ELECTRICITY

The important concept to remember is that the sea represents an all-pervading component that makes up all the realities, and this component we may call the absolute being or pure consciousness.

We may produce ripples or waves in this sea, but, the lower layers of water will never be disturbed; a state of eternal rest will prevail there. We can also compare the size of the ripples or the waves to the different realities we have discussed before and equate the large, coarse waves with the low end of the spectrum of realities, as we show it in Figure 33B. It will correspond to the portion having a low quantity of consciousness and a low-frequency response, while the very fine high-frequency ripples will correspond to the highest level below the absolute.

Let us go now to the very lowest level of matter — a quantum of electricity, a single electron — and ask a physicist what this electron is made of. "Well," he will say, "it's a wave packet having a certain frequency of vibration; the frequency of vibration determines the energy of the electron." Now if we ask what is it that vibrates in this electron or quantum, the answer would be that "no one knows." But if we were to use the analogy of the sea of the absolute, we would visualize the quantum as a packet of ripples on the surface of that sea. It vibrates relative to the calm layers of the infinite sea of pure consciousness, and now we may answer the question as to "what it is that vibrates within the quantum." *It is a unit of pure consciousness that vibrates there.*

Here we have to make a correction of the previous statement, in which I suggested that matter "contains" consciousness. It was used just as a temporary prop, to get you used to thinking of matter as having something to do with consciousness. But now the cat is out of the bag: Matter, being made of quanta of energy, is the vibrating, changing component of pure consciousness. Therefore, we can divide creation into two components, the absolute and the relative. The absolute is fixed, eternal, and invisible, while the relative is the visible, manifest, and *changing aspect.* The latter may be coarse or fine, short-lived or long-lived, but it is always based on the absolute.

By accepting this tenet, we have solved the mind-over-matter problem. The "solution" is that there is no basic difference between the two. We have until now tended to associate mind much more readily with consciousness because mind is abstract and intangible; matter, on the other hand, is solid, hard, hot or cold, and seemingly very different from the mind or consciousness.

When we know that reality is made up of two components, one, an immutable reference line or background, and the other a dynamic, vibrating aspect of the same thing, then we know that both mind and matter are made of the same basic stuff. The difference between them is that we may look at the solid matter as being made up of larger, slower waves or ripples, which implies that it possesses less energy of the absolute and that mind is made up of much finer ripples, which implies that it possesses more of this energy. A good analogy for this would be the different states in which matter is found in Nature: We could compare solid matter to ice and mind or consciousness to steam or vapor, all being the same basic stuff in different form. Both of them are manifest only because they are changing, and this change can be measured against the basic sea of the absolute, which makes up both the ripples and the background. We don't need to wonder now about feats of mind over matter—it is not so much mind "over" matter as mind "over" a different aspect of itself.

We could classify the different realities by the size of their relative components (Fig. 33). We have a large, coarse low frequency wave representing the relative (Fig. 33B), which means that this is a low type of reality; while in Figure 33A, the relative component is very fine, that is, it is of a high frequency and would represent a higher reality, a more refined one—let's say a spiritual reality. We may say this about people as well. All people are made up of relative and absolute components, but some people are more "relative" than others. Let us remember that no matter how relative we are, we are still made of the stuff of the absolute.

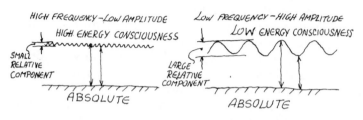

Fig. 33A   **Fig. 33B**

What was the nature of our reality before the vibratory motion started? Clearly, the nonvibratory state is the basis of the latter, which appeared when the vibratory motion arose and became our physical manifest reality. The nonvibratory base we may call the *absolute protospace.*

At the risk of complicating things a little bit, we can also define the absolute as being an *infinitely* fine relative, that is, where the size of the waves is so minute and their frequency so high that they are invisible. When this happens, we have a surface that appears calm and smooth but contains a tremendous energy and *is full of creative potential.* This is the actual definition of the absolute (to the extent that it can be defined); it is a high-energy creative potential plus intelligence. The "intelligence" adds a *self-organizing capability* to any entity in creation. Therefore, the ripples of the "relative" arise in a surface that appears to be smooth but is actually vibrant with potential creative energy. The smaller the amplitude of the waves, the higher the energy contained by the surface. As the waves become so small that the crests and valleys, which are the points of rest, come so close to each other as to overlap, then a state of rest is reached, in which motion is just potential motion and the energy of the system becomes infinitely large.

The absolute is thus a state in which *contrasting concepts become reconciled* and fused. *Movement and rest fuse into one.*

Ours, then, is a vibratory reality — from subnuclear to atomic, to molecular, to macrolevels. *Everything is oscillating between two states of rest.* Everything is producing "sound."

In the next chapter, we shall go with more detail into how consciousness manifests itself in the different realities and how we see this from our vantage point of the scale of evolution.

Summary

We described the evolution of matter in terms of evolution of consciousness. The thrust of evolution is toward more and more complex systems, implying higher and higher levels of consciousness.

Matter forms "live" systems at a certain point along the diagram, which connects quantity to quality of consciousness. The energy-exchange curves give us a measure of our ability to interact with our environment or reality.

The broader our frequency response, the larger the number of realities in which we can function.

An outline of different levels of consciousness or realities includes those above and below the human reality.

The hierarchy of realities is topped by the "absolute." The absolute is the basis of all realities. In its nonmanifest form, it is a potential, intelligent energy. When rippled or modulated, it becomes the basis of our tangible physical matter and individual objects.

6. RELATIVE REALITIES

Mineral reality

Let us start with the lowest realities on our diagram (Fig. 30), and work our way up toward the absolute. Attempt to visualize yourself as a rock. It is difficult, of course, but if we try hard enough to go into the reality of the rock, we may find that one has a dim perception of, say, hot and cold, light and dark. There would be some communication with other rocks, but it would be limited possibly to a dim recognition of the presence of something else. "Social life," of course, would be very limited under these conditions. The important aspect of this situation is that there is no growth, just attrition.

The energy-exchange curve extends into the plant reality and never goes down to zero; that is, it does not touch the vertical line, which means that there is always some energy exchange with other levels.

The plant reality

The first thing we notice as we compare the plant reality to the mineral reality is that in it there is growth and reproduction. There is what we call "life." The quantity of consciousness is higher, and so is the response to stimuli. Naturally, there is adaptation to new conditions, a battle for survival, acute awareness of light and dark. There is a lively "social life" and even sex life — the latter, of course, done discreetly through a third party.

Most of us have heard about experiments demonstrating that plants respond to human emotions — to threats, love, etc. (*The Secret Life of Plants** by Peter Tompkins and Christopher Bird is the best source of information on this subject.) The plant reality is a big jump from the mineral level, but it is relatively static since the ability of plants to move is limited to growth. Note that the energy-exchange curve of plants extends into and beyond the basic frequency range of the human reality.

The animal reality

Here there is a broader span of emotions. There is freedom of movement in three dimensions. There is communication within and across the species. Domesticated animals can communicate with humans. There is a group consciousness in the form of a herd instinct. Some animals are inventive and highly intelligent tool users, not to speak of porpoises, who, judging by the complexity and size of their brains, could rival humans in intelligence.

When we look at Figure 30, we see that the energy-exchange curve of the animal reality extends into the level above the human and into the plant reality, which means that animals can communicate with man and plants. Note that the energy-exchange curve never goes down to zero. There is a minimal and constant awareness on the part of beings belonging to one reality of those of the other realities. This is so because the common uniting element of all creation is consciousness, and through this bridge all things are in constant contact, as we shall see later.

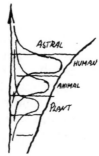

* New York: Harper and Row, 1973; London: Allen Lane, 1974.

The human reality

We all know the human reality, but what probably most of us don't know about it is that human consciousness can be taught to expand and learn how to interact with the whole spectrum of realities we have described in our diagram. This is the real meaning of the phrase "expansion of consciousness." It means that our cerebrospinal nervous system is capable of being developed to such a point that we can tune in on any of these realities, from the very lowest mineral to the very highest spiritual levels. The expression "development of the nervous system," then, as used in this book, is synonymous with the expansion of consciousness.

Much has been said about the effects of drugs on the expansion of consciousness. These drugs do not expand the consciousness; rather, they alter it and tend to funnel it into particular levels. These levels may be either above or below the human reality shown in our diagram. "Bad trips" means that consciousness is projected into a reality below the human, and is naturally experienced as a nightmarish reality.

Sometimes consciousness is projected into realities above ours; then one has a "good trip." However, all these experiences are necessarily distorted because the drug prevents the brain from functioning normally. Also, there is little control over the events or levels one happens to enter. The only positive thing about these drugs is that they do show us that we see our reality through a tiny window, that there is much more to it. On the other hand, prolonged use of drugs will destroy the ability of the nervous system to evolve normally in the direction toward the higher levels shown in our diagram by the arrow of evolution. This is due to the instability in the nervous system produced by the long-term use of drugs.* In order to interact on a certain level of consciousness or reality, the mind has to be very steady and clear.

By now it will be no surprise to you that we use the terms "realities" and "levels of consciousness" as interchangeable concepts. We hope to show that realities are states of consciousness, as we go deeper into the chapter, by taking examples from well-known literature on the subject.

In the last few years, several excellent books have appeared on just this subject by several authors, among them those by Carlos Castaneda.† In reading his books, one gets a good idea of what we mean by "communication across different realities." Animals and plants or plant gods communicate with humans. The spirits of the water, of the rocks, etc., are all very active, and we begin to understand the level of consciousness at which all this activity takes place. It is clear enough that the sorcerer operates mostly in the plant and animal realities. Throughout the Castaneda books, the general feeling is that one is in constant danger: "If you do this — you will get killed, if you do that — you survive." One is a "warrior" in that he either kills or gets killed. This is the animal reality, the survival instinct in operation. Beings of this reality lack the knowledge of the higher realities; therefore, we find not once the words "love" or "God" mentioned in the first three books by Castaneda. This knowledge appears higher up on the scale of evolution. In his *Tales of Power*, however, we do find that the master sorcerers Don Juan and Don Genaro have the knowledge of higher realities reaching into and probably above the causal level. They manage to "split" Castaneda and demonstrate to him his two components: the reasoning, material "personality" on the one hand; and the pure awareness, on the other. Love appears in Don Genaro as love for the earth, the mass of mineral matter that has an enormous amount of consciousness. This big being reciprocates his love by bestowing on him unusual powers.

* This, I believe, is so in most cases.
† *The Teachings of Don Juan.* New York: Ballantine Books, 1969; Harmondsworth: Penguin, 1970. *A Separate Reality.* New York: Simon & Schuster, 1971; London: Bodley Head, 1971. *Journey to Ixtlan.* New York: Simon & Schuster, 1972; London Bodley Head, 1973.

Perhaps it would be proper at this time to explain the strange entities we have just mentioned — the plant god or spirit and the spirits of the rocks, water, etc., that appear in Castaneda's books and in the folklore of many peoples. We are now armed with the knowledge of the absolute, and we know that matter represents consciousness of a certain quantity and quality, but those who still have difficulty with this concept may keep the idea that matter "contains" a certain amount of consciousness.

Particle-wave duality

We shall now look at the possible mechanism behind these phenomena. The principle of particle-wave duality holds not only in the limited area of photons, electrons, or nuclear particles but also in the larger aggregates of matter. By this duality we understand, for example, that light can be represented as a field of radiation, but when our eyes or instruments interact with this field, they sense this radiation in the form of little bullets or photons, the individual particles of light. Thus, we have a field of continuous electromagnetic radiation, which has a wave-like character, but which we see neither with our eyes nor with instruments. It becomes manifest to us only when it hits our retina, but when it does so, it behaves like single, discrete particles known as photons.

It may be worthwhile to ponder this. It sounds quite similar to our discussion of how the relative or manifest arises from the absolute. The absolute is analogous to the smooth field of radiation, but in order to manifest and become visible, it has to raise ripples on its surface; it has to become quantized or granulated, which makes its surface visible.

WAVE PACKET

In our example of the light, the radiation field became manifest as particles (photons) only when it interacted with our retina. A process of *individuation* of the continuum occurred, which made it possible for our senses to interact with the light. We propose that this process of individuation or particle-wave duality holds true, as mentioned before, on a much larger scale in Nature.

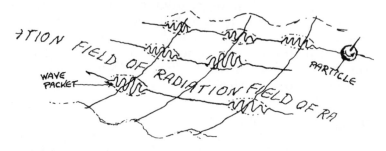

The construction and maintenance of a nature spirit

Let us now picture this principle in action and see whether we can explain or, even better, design and make a Nature spirit or even a minor god of the elements in Nature. First of all, we have to pick a continuum. Let us take a smooth valley. Suppose that there is a big rock formation projecting prominently from this valley. We now have an individuum. It is definitely separate from the valley, although we see it only in contrast to the valley.

We know that matter is consciousness (or, if you prefer, *contains* consciousness). This consciousness, if there is enough of it (a critical mass), will develop a dim awareness of self. Over millions of years this dim awareness may be strengthened into a sharper identity, possibly through interaction with other creatures. If an animal finds a hiding

place in the rock formation, it will feel grateful to the rock for its shelter, and the rock will feel it. And its (ego) will be boosted if a bird comes and makes a nest and lays eggs in it. The bird's evolving life and consciousness, which is higher than that of the rock, will give its consciousness a push upward. Sooner or later the consciousness of the rock will evolve into a "spirit of the rock." By now he has learned that if he extends protection to these creatures, they respond with grateful feelings. Slowly, therefore, be begins to understand that this business is to protect them. Soon he becomes quite adept at this and will attract more creatures. In short, he is in business. Being in close contact with live beings will speed his evolution, so to speak, and widen his range of responses. He will have a relatively low-frequency response, corresponding to that of the mineral level of consciousness, but in this case he will be at the very top of the band delineating the mineral consciousness. He will border on the plant consciousness, and his energy-exchange curve will reach into that of the astral region. So when a human being finally comes to this rock, one who is sensitive to Nature, he will feel that there is something special about the rock. It produces some particular feeling in him either of protection or repulsion.

Let this remain between us — a spirit such as this is still quite unevolved and stupid, and he may want to show off his prowess to man by producing some silly trick. When this happens, the man, if he has noticed it, will become duly

impressed. Some other people will come around who have heard about the happenings around the rock. They will also witness the tricks, and pretty soon there is a cult going. This boosts the ego of the spirit of the rock immensely because the thoughts of the people who concentrate on him add to his power.

Let us look for a moment at the effect of thoughts on things or people. A thought is energy that causes the neurons in the brain to fire in a certain pattern. That naturally produces tiny currents along definite paths in the brain cortex that can be picked up with sensitive instruments through electrodes on the surface of the skull. In other words, a thought that starts out as a tiny stir eventually develops into a full-fledged thought producing at least a 70 milivolt potential somewhere in the cortex. It fires the first neuron, which in turn causes others to fire in a certain sequence. However, in this universe no energy is lost. If we can pick up the current produced by the thought outside the head, it means that the energy of the thought was broadcast in the form of electromagnetic waves, and at the velocity of light into the environment and, finally, into the cosmos.

Now this is serious business, especially since thought energy can be focused. As long as we are just sitting and producing idle thoughts, the thought energy is diffuse, and it eventually spreads out, weakens, and disappears. However, when we consciously concentrate and send coherent thoughts, that thought energy or thought form will impinge on the person for whom the thought was meant. We shall discuss this in more detail later.

Now back to our "spirit of the rock." We have said that when people concentrate on him, it adds immensely to his capability to do things because he is stimulated by the level of energy produced by the human nervous system. He is hobnobbing with royalty. From here on, everything is snowballing. He will be able to pull off more impressive tricks, which will impress primitive people, and eventually they will bring him sacrifices to draw him to their side. Or, if they feel that he may be angered by their activity within his jurisdiction, they will sacrifice to him in order to appease him. It is known that miners in copper mines of Peru sacrifice llamas to the spirit of the mine every year with great pomp and ceremony. According to the miners, this spirit, who is the individuated consciousness of a vein of copper, will be appeased by this sacrifice and not harm or cause accidents to the people working in the mine, who, in effect, are digging up and diminishing his body.

Eventually, the "spirit of the rock," which started out as a vague, dim awareness in a mass of matter, develops into a powerful spirit or a tribal god. Now that we have successfully followed the spirit's evolution, we may have a slightly better insight into the meaning of Mescalito, the spirit of the peyote plant described by Carlos Castaneda in *The Teachings of Don Juan*. We are dealing here with a more evolved entity, representing the sum total of consciousness of all the peyote plants in a certain area — in other words, their group consciousness. These are plants having a relatively high level of consciousness, certainly higher than that of a rock. Mescalito, therefore, is more intelligent and has a greater variety of responses than the spirit of the rock. He is in constant contact with humans, who view him as an "ally." They cater to him, and he responds by performing for them in his own way. At first, he was nothing more than a space charge, a cloud of low consciousness. As he gained energy, he may have developed a more definite form, a shadowy one at first. Later, when human consciousness interacted with him, he may have resonated to human thoughts and formed himself a body that matched their expectations and that could be visible to such sensitive people as the clairvoyants.

More on individuation

In a way, all these minor gods or Nature spirits rely on the energy they get from others to keep themselves powerful. Just like the politicians, their power and influence depends on the size and the strength of their constituency. Eventually, as their constituency diminishes, they fade from the scene, as did the gods of the ancient peoples, for example, the Baal, the Moloch, the Greek and Roman gods, etc. They remain just at some nominal value, sufficient to hold a social security card for old-age pension.

Now that we have become quite proficient at analyzing and synthesizing gods, we can give a quick try and see whether we can come up with a handy god who operates the local weather.

An air mass is/has consciousness. There is a big general pattern of winds on a global scale such as the trade winds. That mass of air would be represented by a very large, substantial entity, of the level of consciousness corresponding to the mineral level. He, in turn, will delegate responsibility for the local weather to smaller entities *contained within him* who know the local needs. These entities will do their best to keep everybody happy under the given conditions.

A tornado is a typical high-energy individuation of a mass of air. A hurricane is another. You may remember that before we started analyzing gods in such a down-to-earth manner, we talked about particle-wave duality or individuation. A tornado or a Nature spirit is a good demonstration of such individuation. This holds true throughout all levels of Nature, all the way to the absolute. So that we can say that Nature is modular. The very biggest entity, the universe, contains smaller entities, which contain smaller entities, which contain still smaller entities — and so on ad infinitum. The term "modular" means that a unit will always be divided into smaller but integral units.

The communications gap

Reading this, do you get the feeling that you are standing on an island, and there is a lot of action around you, but that you are somehow blindfolded because you don't seem to see any of this action? Well, unfortunately, that's the truth about us humans.

We have seen how the mineral consciousness can extend into the reality above that of our normal waking reality or state of consciousness, the so-called astral reality. Admittedly, Figure 30 is a rather simplified attempt to express in two dimensions aspects of consciousness that are multidimensional. Not everything is as smooth as the diagram shows. However, it is a good preliminary device that allows us to put these complex things into some sort of order.

Let us look at the level of consciousness or reality above our human waking state. It may be of interest to note that we humans do go quite often into the next level above us, the so-called astral level. In fact, we appear there during our dreaming episodes every night, especially during the REM periods* of active dreaming, which occur about five times a night. In these periods, we are pursuing activities that are often emotionally charged. (We often find that in REM

* REM or rapid eye movement sleep is characterized by active eye movements, but at the same time, a completely limp body. The eyes seem to be following some lively action. These periods are repeated about every 90 to 100 minutes for about 5 to 7 minutes.

dreams we encounter people and animals, which means that they do reach into that level of consciousness, as the energy-exchange curve shows. They act either as props or are actively participating in our dream situations.) What is typical to this level of consciousness is that our mental-rational self seems to be absent here. We are quite content to put up with situations that we could not tolerate in our waking reality. Suppose that we are dreaming of a green horse talking on the telephone in a public telephone booth. In our dream, this would probably not disturb us in the least. We would not react with our reason, saying: "No, this could not be," but we would sense that this is a nice horse, he does not threaten us in any way and that there is nothing wrong with a horse talking on the telephone. In short, we would react to this situation emotionally and not try to reason and figure out how he ever got that dime into the pay phone.

The astral realities

Note that all the lower realities we have mentioned before appear on the astral level. The astral is a vast reality that serves as a bridge connecting all "physical" realities — the mineral, the vegetable, the animal, and the human with or without physical bodies. During our waking state, we don't usually function there, but there are good descriptions by people who can go into the astral reality at will, and who have taught themselves to function there quite well.

We have talked about the books by Castaneda in which he mentions the "dreaming" of himself into another self that acted independently of him. Robert A. Monroe's *Journeys Out of the Body* (*op. cit.*) deals exclusively with so-called astral travel. Again, we see here that the functioning on the astral level is dominated by emotion.

Why does Nature cause us to operate in the astral plane during our sleep? We know that the arrow of evolution is pointing in the direction from the physical to the astral level. According to our diagram, we see that all matter will be moving through these levels under the pressure of evolution. What Nature is doing to us during sleep is simply giving us a "preview of coming events," just like in a movie theater. In this way Nature gradually acquaints us with functioning on our next level in order to prevent the shock of a sudden adjustment when we finally move there for a more extended stay, the so-called death. Figure 34A shows an enlarged portion of Figure 30 dealing with this matter. This is a very simplified diagram. It does not take into account the beings that move much faster than the average along the evolutionary path, those who engage in spiritual practices. It shows that an average person presently spans at least three levels of consciousness, that is, the physical, the astral, and the mental. Each coil in the helix represents many "life-death" cycles.

SUCCESSIVE LIFE CYCLES

Fig. 34A

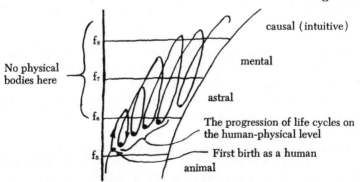

As an example, let us follow the life of a person born into the lower portion of human physical reality. "Lower" does not mean a lower economical status, rather a person having a rather undeveloped nervous system in terms of evolution of consciousness and his ability to interact with the higher levels — in other words, a purely materialistic human.

When such a person dies, he also appears on the correspon-
dingly low level of the astral plane. This is the "slum area"
of the astral region, the nearest in its frequency response to
the physical. Therefore, the interaction between it and the
physical level is easy. Such psychic phenomena as polter-
geists, haunting spooks, Ouija board personalities, possess-
ing spirits, etc., all belong in this general low-level category.
This is the meaning of the cross-hatched triangle formed by
the crossing of the two energy-exchange curves in Figure
34B.

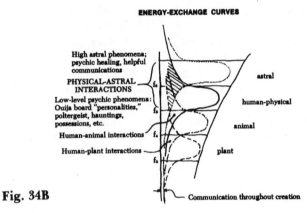

ENERGY-EXCHANGE CURVES

High astral phenomena;
psychic healing, helpful
communications

PHYSICAL-ASTRAL
INTERACTIONS

Low-level psychic phenomena:
Ouija board "personalities,"
poltergeist, hauntings,
possessions, etc.

Human-animal interactions

Human-plant interactions

astral

human-physical

animal

plant

Communication throughout creation

Fig. 34B

Now notice that a rising helix connects the human with
the astral levels (Fig. 34). This helix starts at the lower level
of human evolution. The entity "dies," lives for a while in
the lower astral region; then, provided he has made enough
progress, he is reborn on a slightly higher level of human
existence.

I am suggesting here, as you have noticed, that the "dead"
are not quite as dead as most of us like to think they are.
Many eyebrows are probably being raised at this point
because we have reached a touchy and controversial subject
— that of reincarnation. It is not that until now we discussed only nice, tame subjects, but these subjects were presented as speculative issues. In other words, we discussed
them on the mental level. In contrast, the issue of reincarnation has an emotional impact on many people.

To those readers who need a more objective approach to reincarnation, we suggest reading a booklet called "Deathbed Observations by Physicians and Nurses"* by Carlis Osis, and books by Ian Stevenson (*20 Suggestions of Reincarnation*†) and Raymond A. Moody, Jr. (*Life After Life.*‡) In the meantime, we shall continue with our rising helix.

The human unit of consciousness will, we hope, be reborn next time around on a higher level at each turn of the helix. By the time he has learned all there is to learn on the physical level of evolution, he will move into the astral region and will not come back into the physical existence. That is, he will not need a physical body any more but will continue to live in the astral realities, which will be as real and as solid to him as our level is to us. The reason for this, naturally, is that the energy exchange with his environment is maximum in that reality. A nice thing in the astral reality is one's ability to manipulate time. Time becomes pliable and subjective. The astral realities lie in the region between our timelike universe and the spacelike universe described in Chapter 4.

To readers who are still having problems digesting the above statements, we suggest that they check them out for themselves by raising their level of consciousness to the point at which they will be able to function on the astral levels. This is relatively easy to do, but it does require time. There are many meditative techniques that will take them there; however, one has to be very careful not to go off unprotected into the astral plane. As we mentioned before, the boundary layer between the physical and the astral is populated by creatures of the lowest type: criminals, drunks, etc. That one has no physical body and is "dead" does not change one's personality or intelligence. These will attack the unsuspecting tourist; therefore, the protection of an experienced teacher is required before attempting forays

---

* Parapsychology Foundation, Inc., 29 West Fifty-seventh St., New York, N.Y. 10019.
† Charlottesville, Va.: University of Virginia Press, 1974.
‡ New York: Bantam Books, 1976.

into the unknown. Going unprotected would be the equivalent of entering blindfolded some tough neighborhood in a large city. One would get mugged, beaten, and robbed within the first few minutes of the experiment.

The mental reality

Once the human unit of consciousness has worked out its emotional problems, evolution leads it into the mental levels of consciousness. You have probably noticed in Figure 34 that as one "dies" in the astral, one's helix takes him into the mental reality. There is a lot of energy exchanged between the two levels; they are not exclusive, and entities from the higher astral level may tour the mental regions. Again, this reality is solid to its inhabitants. The big difference between the physical and non-physical realities is the ability to create one's environment instantly by the power of thought or desire. This is actually happening on the physical plane as well, but it takes much longer, and much more thinking and doing are required before a change in our environment can occur. A good popular description of the mental realities and our reality, as seen from the mental levels, are two books by Jane Roberts: *Seth Speaks* and *Nature of Personal Reality*.* In these realities the human unit has overcome its tendency to act emotionally, which is an inheritance going back to the animal level. On the mental level the balanced mind and the search for practical or theoretical knowledge are dominant. The only emotion allowed at this level is love.

The causal (intuitive) reality

After hundreds, perhaps thousands of life cycles, we may find ourselves in the causal level. While before, on the mental levels, the search for knowledge was foremost, here knowledge seems to come easily. That is why this reality is called the intuitive level. Here knowledge comes in a nonlinear

* Englewood Cliffs, N.J.: Prentice-Hall, 1972 and 1974, respectively.

way. Before, we had to learn a subject by stringing together pieces of information one at a time. Here knowledge comes in large chunks, imprinted on the mind in a fraction of a second. Sometimes it comes in a simple diagrammatic form or in symbolic forms. After the imprinting, the mind analyzes the information, if needed, in the usual way, that is, if there is a need to translate this knowledge into normal human knowledge on the physical level.

The inhabitants of that region do not need to translate such knowledge into a linear form as we know it and have a total understanding of the information contained in these condensed symbols.

The creative process

We may now understand the creative insights of artists, scientists, and inventors who rely on these chunks of intuitive knowledge for progress in their fields. Such moments of insight are known to come after a person has saturated himself with detailed knowledge of all the possible avenues that may lead to the solution of his problem. However, all he has is a clutter of detail with no elegant and economical pattern connecting them. Then, suddenly, in a moment of relaxation, when least expected, it is as if the sky has opened for a second, and the solution to the problem comes. It is received as a chunk, all of it, all details visible and fitting together in an elegant order. It may be the culmination of years of search, and it is all imprinted on the mind in the intuitive flash. The information is imprinted on the mind and then is decoded in our normal linear fashion, while the person is still in a state of joyous ecstasy. What has actually happened is that in a relaxed moment, when the mind was not busying itself with any problem in particular or may have been in a state of reverie, it projected itself into the intuitive or causal levels for a very short period of time, as described in Chapter

4. Here the unit of consciousness saw the solution since solutions to all problems are already present in the spacelike universe (as will be explained in the chapter on cosmology). In other words, the solution was received when the mind momentarily happened to be in an altered state of consciousness. In that state, the subjective time had expanded so that there was enough time to search out and retain the solution. In short, the mind was resonated with that high level for a while and was able to absorb the available information. This kind of experience naturally makes the recipient very excited. He feels that he has experienced something mystical out of the ordinary — and indeed he has. The feeling that:— " . . . time has come to a stop . . ." is a very common experience in this case.

This is Nature's way of communicating with its favourite creatures, the creative people of all walks of life.

The other bodies

It would be good at this point to sum up what we have so far discussed about the levels of consciousness.

We have seen how a bundle of consciousness or the human unit of consciousness is slowly moving under the pressure of evolution in the direction of higher complexity; of more knowledge; of higher interaction and a better understanding of nature; and therefore, as the energy-exchange curve shows, toward more control over one's environment and more happiness.

In Chapter 2, which deals with the microrealities, we have seen that the physical body is made up of interacting, pulsating energy fields. What we call a "physical body" — flesh, bones, and blood — rapidly disappears when highly magnified. A physical body, therefore, or any piece of matter, can be viewed as an interference pattern of electromagnetic fields that changes with the passage of time. However, regardless of how tenuous our physical bodies may look under high magnification, they seem to serve us quite well as they interact with our physical environment.

Let us see whether we can carry this a little further. Are there any chances of finding or inventing other "bodies" that would serve us as well in interactions with the other higher realities? The answer is yes. Interacting wave patterns will inevitably contain higher harmonics. In a less technical language, suppose we strike one of the strings of a grand piano and produce a middle C note; the string then vibrates at 264 Hz. Assume now that the cover of the piano is lifted, and we have an unobstructed view of the strings. We shall notice right away that the eighth string (including the C that was struck), and counting up the scale, will vibrate quite strongly in harmony with the C string. The eighth string is a full octave higher, which means that it vibrates exactly at double the rate of the first C at 528 Hz. We find that other strings also vibrate in resonance. The string half an octave higher then the middle C, which is the note G, will vibrate at 396 Hz., not quite as strongly as the previous string. Other strings will be found to vibrate even less.

We can see that the strings that are separated by integral multiples of their vibratory rates, like 2 times, 3 times, etc., resonate best, while where the ratio becomes fractional, like 1½ or 11/3 times the original frequency, the exchange of energy with the original string is not as good.

Let us go back to our vibrating bodies. We see now that we can make a reasonable assumption for the existence of "bodies" made up of the higher harmonics of our physical body. They may not look exactly like our physical bodies, and they may be outside the reach of our instruments and normal senses. We can also take these higher harmonic bodies and divide them into arbitrary groups. We can say that bodies vibrating within such and such a range of frequencies will be called the "astral bodies." They will help us to interact on the astral level. Next would be bodies containing higher harmonics, which will allow us to interact on the mental level, etc. Successively higher harmonics of our physical body, then, will allow us to interact with higher and higher realities. These bodies will not interact well with our matter and will be normally invisible to us because of weak interaction between them and the physical body.

To summarize, we have seen that the physical body is an instrument that allows us to interact best with our physical environment. This body is interpenetrated by "bodies" or fields having higher vibratory rates. They extend beyond the limits of the physical body (Fig. 35). This is what clairvoyants can perceive as colorful egg-shaped halos or auras surrounding our physical bodies. They contain a lot of information about us for those who can properly read the meaning of the colors, size, shape, and motion of these bodies. The most strongly visible of them would be the astral body because of the nearness of its vibratory scale to the physical. It is visible at about 18 to 24 inches from the physical body.

There is another "body" we should mention here, and that is the so-called "health aura." It is really an extension of the physical body and is made up of a cloud of particles given off by the physical body, such as the tiny salt crystals, small flakes of dry skin (keratin), molecules of water, ammonia, CO_2, etc. We assume that this soup of particles gets excited by the bombardment of ultraviolet photons given off in small quantities by the skin, possibly due to mitotic radiation.* Hence, we have a soup of charged, ionized particles around the body that seems to be limited quite sharply on its periphery. This field is very sensitive to the state of our health, and hence its name: "the health aura."

It is possible for us to say at this point, without causing much consternation, that Figure 19 in Chapter 2, which showed how the static field produced by the body changes with distance from the body, is actually a representation of the health aura and the "astral body."

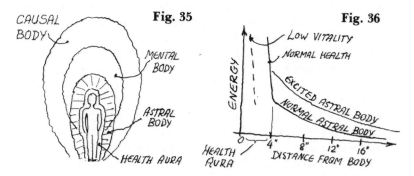

Fig. 35   Fig. 36

* Ultraviolet radiation given off during the division of cells.

You will recall from Chapter 2 that the 4-inch limit of the almost vertical leg of the curve is very sensitive to the person's vitality level or state of health. Also, when a person is emotionally excited, the flat leg of the curve will increase in potential and rise about 30 per cent above the normal level. This means that the emotional (astral) body has been excited to a higher level of activity (Fig. 36).

You may have noticed that our higher bodies seem to be equated with the electrostatic potential about us. This isn't quite so. The electrostatic field is just one small component of these higher harmonic bodies, which fortunately we can measure and identify. The other components in which most of the energy of these bodies lies will have to await the development of new and different kinds of instrumentation.

Putting it all together

We have described a set of bodies made of higher harmonics of the physical body, which interpenetrate our physical body. This mechanism allows us to interact on different levels of consciousness. A few examples may make this clearer.

The basic underlying function of our physical and other bodies is to pick up signals or stimuli, process them, and respond to them. That is what makes up our daily experiences. Suppose now that we visualize ourselves as a radio-like device that is receiving four or five different stations simultaneously. One station will by far overshadow the others in loudness, and among the others there are also differences in their degree of loudness. We can liken the strongest station to the physical reality. Whatever comes in through this channel is heard most strongly, while the other "stations" representing the astral, mental, causal, and spiritual realities are successively weaker. Thus, people whose ears are not very sensitive will hear only the physical station, while people with more refined hearing will hear more of the weaker stations. The important thing to realize is that we are capable of listening to all the stations simultaneously. Our listening to the weaker stations would improve considerably if we could only turn off the loud physical station. This is what we do in sleep, in meditation, or in sensory-deprivation chambers. That the loud physical station is on does not mean that we don't pick up what the other stations are broadcasting. Take, for instance, the sudden attraction or aversion we feel for someone whom we meet for the first time. We pick this up through our emotional band. In the case of a sudden attraction, our astral bodies, which extend beyond the physical, resonated in harmony; in the case of aversion, strong dissonances must have been produced.

Finally, we come to subliminal stimuli. For example, a constant irritation with something or someone on any of these levels may appear as a change in the physical body, as psychosomatic illness. Repressed anger, being a powerful emotion, may cause cancer in some people; anxiety and uncertainty will cause ulcers in others. Frustration on the mental level may seep down into the physical level as depression, etc.

The weakest station is the spiritual. This is the little voice that tells what is right and what is wrong, the voice of our higher self, our conscience.

Sometimes we meet people with whom we share a common way of thinking, almost to a point at which, when confronted with a situation, we can predict their reasoning step by step and, as a result, their reaction to the given situation. Here we seem to resonate on the mental level, which is quite enjoyable.

The intuitive "gut" feeling about success or failure of a project, for instance, is picked up through our intuitive band. When we find that two or more artists, scientists, or inventors have come up with an identical idea at approximately the same time, we can assume that they all tapped the causal intuitive level, where the idea happened to be waiting for them, and they resonated with it.

The brain

We have by now become acquainted with a profusion of bodies, but our brains seem to have been lost in the shuffle. Let me suggest that the brain is a piece of hardware, a computer terminal, which normally processes the input provided by the sense in the waking state. When the input from the senses is not processed, as in deep sleep, this piece of hardware is in a state of complete rest and is not generating any images. However, as soon as our consciousness becomes focused in the astral during the dreaming cycles, information from that reality will pour in, and the imagery of the action produced in the brain will be followed by movements of the eyes and sometimes limbs.

An experiment with the brain

It would be useful to try a little experiment with our brains. Let us sit down in a comfortable position in a quiet place and try to stop our thinking process for a while. You may find that this is quite a difficult job. To make the task a little easier for you, I suggest that you visualize your senses turned inside your head, that is, that your eyes should be looking into your head, your ears should be listening to what is going on inside the head, and your senses are bundled up in the center of your head. Try to keep your mind blank. You will find that without noticing, you have been thinking. Try to see whether you can follow a thought all the way back to its origin. You may find that what later becomes a full-blown thought starts out at first as a tiny little impulse. This impulse grows and grows and eventually develops into a thought that is recognizable. This implies that we are thinking on a level on which thought is not yet formulated.

For those who can quiet their minds as a result of long years of practicing meditation, a thought is a very coarse, big thing. It's like a truck rumbling through the head and disturbs the very fine equilibrium achieved by balancing the mind in a nonthought state. I suggest, therefore, that our brain is not the *source* of thought but a *thought amplified*.

As we have seen, it takes a tiny impulse, magnifies it for us, and only then does it become a thought. It appears that the thought does not originate within the brain; rather, the brain picks up the tiny impulses implanted there by our astral, mental, or causal bodies. These couple very weakly with the physical brain and therefore at first can produce only a very weak signal in the brain. It is the function of the brain to amplify this signal for us into a useful form.

Summary

Nature or, in the broadest sense of the word, creation, is made up of a continuous spectrum of realities.

Present mankind happens to function most of the time in what we call the physical reality, but we also function to a certain extent within four or five of our neighboring realities as well.

One can train oneself to interact in these other realities by using certain available techniques.

Our successful interaction with these other realities depends on the extent to which we have developed our vehicles or bodies, which are matched to respond to the frequency span of each reality.

These bodies are analogous to the higher harmonics of our physical bodies and contain all the information accumulated over many lifetimes.

These higher bodies are centered most of the time about the physical body, but they can also move and function independently of it.

At the transition called death, the higher bodies that make up our so-called "personalities" leave the physical body and continue their existence on the levels above the physical, which are to the unit of consciousness as valid a reality as the physical was previously. This unit of consciousness can still interact weakly with the physical reality.

Thoughts or desires do not originate in the brain. They are generated by the respective bodies or fields that act on the brain to produce tiny impulses that the brain amplifies into thoughts. "Thought" exists below the threshold of a recognizable thought.

7. THE PARABLE OF THE BICYCLE

It may indeed be difficult for many of the readers to accept what has been said until now. I would like to remind them that meaningful breakthroughs in science, art, and technology come not by "figuring out" things to the nth degree but through intuitive leaps or insight, which are later rationalized. As mentioned before, when operating in unchartered territory, intuition is the only thing we can rely on. Take as an example entrepreneurs. In making decisions, these people rely to a great extent on their intuition or "gut feeling," as they call it. The reason for this is that the number of variables to be considered in each decision is just too great to handle, and with conditions constantly changing, it is simply impossible to figure things out completely. So they rely on their intuitive input. They will say that that decision "felt right," that they knew that things would work out for the best.

Now, considering how large a component of our civilization is constituted by business, we should, perhaps, have a little more respect for intuition.

We have suggested before that the material we have discussed until now is self-validating. This means that anybody who is willing to make the effort can find out about these things himself and confirm them for himself.

Let me use as an example the bicycle. Suppose that we show a bicycle to someone who has never seen one and try to convince him that it is a safe and practical conveyance. He will think that we are joking since it is clear through observation that the bicycle is a highly unstable contraption. Clearly, no amount of explaining will help, and only after learning how to ride it (and that includes an ample number of bruised knees and elbows) will our subject be convinced of the merits of the bicycle. In other words, only after having gone through the subjective experience is he ready to start using the bicycle and even begin to persuade others of its merits. He recognizes that in his previous thinking he missed an important point, and that was the *invisible* principle of inertia that keeps the bicycle upright when in motion.

Sooner or later, science will have to come around and use this method in evaluating things that are "invisible," subjective, but nevertheless reproducible. We can visualize the possibility of asking a group of one hundred people to put themselves into a certain well-defined level of consciousness and have them describe their experiences. If the majority of the subjects independently describe similar experiences, and these are reproducible, then we may have to admit that we are dealing with real states common to all, thus establishing a fact.

Experiments of this kind are conducted today by the so-called biofeedback experimenters; by those who study hypnosis and altered states of consciousness; and, last but not least, the drug companies. The only way to find out how psychoactive drugs affect the system is to give the drug to people and ask them to describe their reactions to the experiences with the drug. There is no objective way to measure such subtle effects. The reported experience of the majority of people who have taken the drug is fed back to the chemists, who can then modify the drug accordingly.

Let us go back to Chapter 4. In the experiment with time we offered evidence that it is really not very difficult to function consciously in the reality next to ours. Those readers who managed to slow down or stop the watch altogether have actually projected themselves and stayed for a while, fully aware, in the so-called astral reality. Let us analyze what happened.

In the instructions, it was suggested that you transport all your sensory and reasoning apparatus to a different point in space and time — to "the beach." When this is properly performed, your physical body has for all practical purposes displayed a temporary "death"; that is, your physical eyes did not register the physical reality around you (nor would your ears). Your senses were registering a different reality, which occurred in the *past*. Therefore, you have experienced a tilting of your subjective space-time coordinates by a certain angle $\ddagger$ to the objective frame of reference. To those who managed to slow down time by a certain amount, the angle $\ddagger$ was somewhere between 0 and 90 degrees, while for those who managed to "stop" time almost completely, the angle came close to 90 degrees. At that point their subjective space axes were pointing into the objective *past*, and the subjective time axis into objective *space*, while objective time required for the operation was diminishing rapidly. Therefore, persons who managed almost to "stop" time (these will be invariably creative types) could not only go to a nearby beach but to any place in the universe within the time that it would have taken them to visualize their destination. This is because they have projected their sensing and reasoning apparatus or their "observer" at practically infinite velocities to the wanted destination. It is creative *visualization* that can take them there.

In short, the ingredients most helpful for being able to function in the different realities are, as we have mentioned before, creative visualization and a steady mind. Whether we achieve these levels or not depends on the extent of development and refinement of our nervous system, which determines the extent to which we can expand our consciousness and how far we can range in levels beyond the physical. Such development can be achieved only by meditative techniques. Sometimes, though such development may occur spontaneously, or due to some accident, a person will tend to become unbalanced, because of his inability to distinguish between the physical and the new realities he can suddenly see. He will eventually be diagnosed as schizophrenic, because he will see or hear things which a "normal" person does not see or hear.

"The observer"

We have come to a point at which we can define in more familiar terms our "observer." We see from all that was said before that the traveling, mobile entity is our sensing-feeling apparatus or astral body and the reasoning apparatus — the one that can interpret the events — our mental body. When the individual is well developed, he can utilize his causal or intuitive body as well. If we put these three together, we may find that the best way to describe these elements is to call them our psyche. This psyche is independent of the body but uses the body as a kind of garage in which it stays most of the time. The more traditional name for the psyche is the "soul."

The psyche serves as a bridge between the physical level and our real selves — spiritual beings, who operate on the physical level through the mediation of the psyche. The distance between the spiritual entity, which we can call the "higher self," and our physical reality, in terms of quality of consciousness, is so large that the spirit could not directly operate a normal physical body. It needs this intermediary between psyche or soul to do the job. The spiritual level is the highest shown in Figure 30. It is the bridge to the absolute.

The spiritual level

It is unfortunate that the word "spirit" or "spirits" in the English language is so versatile. It is used to denote the liquid kind of spirits and to describe discarnate entities as well — that is, people without physical bodies and spooks of all kinds, from the benign, garden variety to vicious, malevolent, degenerate entities. We shall use the word "spirit" or "spiritual" to describe the highest level of human evolution (Fig. 30), which borders on the absolute. It is very difficult to draw any sharp demarcation lines because the very highest spiritual merges into the absolute, which is the level of the Creators. It is, therefore, directly connected with the knowledge and the structure of the universe and the cosmos.

As you may remember from the description of the causal level, knowledge comes as chunks of information, not in linear, sequential form, as we normally absorb knowledge. Take, for example, the way we look at a picture: Our eyes scan it in a zigzag fashion, and so bit by bit we take in the information contained in the picture. In the causal region and above it, the picture would have been imprinted on us as if our whole body would make contact with it in a flash, like an instant contact print. We would realize the picture in all its miniscule detail in an instant and then have plenty of time to contemplate its meaning. The same system of gaining knowledge holds true in the spiritual realms.

Individual interests naturally vary, and so will the information imparted to them on all levels. If someone's interest lies in cosmology, he will probably obtain information on the structure of the universe and the cosmos in as much detail as he can comprehend at the moment. The important thing to realize is that the universe, through its incentive system, which we call evolution, is anxious to impart as much knowledge as possible to its sentient beings in order to allow them to move as fast as possible along the evolutionary ladder and develop their consciousness to the highest possible degree. The universe wants to make itself known to those who can comprehend its language, and that language becomes more and more intelligible to us as our spiritual component unfolds.

Now let us make it clear: "Spiritual" does not mean that it has anything to do with religion as we know it. (Religious leaders are sometimes called spiritual leaders.) It has to do only with the development and refinement of the nervous system and the accompanying rise in the level of consciousness, which has reached a point in frequency high enough on the scale of the quality of consciousness to resonate with the highest levels of creation. This automatically entails the development of inner moral values and the development of the heart. By this we mean that a person on that level of development will automatically tend to help people in need and will radiate an energy that on the physical level is expressed as the emotion called "love." We would define love as energy and not an emotion since emotions are confined to the physical and astral levels of reality. Beyond those levels emotions are not encountered. Therefore, what we call "love" is an energy or radiation that pervades the whole cosmos. It is possibly the basis of what we know as the phenomenon of gravitation.

To function on this level is the goal of all yoga training. The word "yoga" means union, by which is meant union with the absolute. An accomplished yogi is able to function on all levels of creation; to describe events in the past and future; and, because the energy-exchange curve is very high on this level, he is able to influence Nature in a positive way. Eventually, he becomes a factor stimulating evolution of mankind and of the planet.

In this chapter we have been singing praises to the spiritual level of consciousness and the rewards of those who achieve it. But this does not mean that the universe is spiritual. The universe just *is*. However, what we call spiritual development is the key to achieving a subjective and objective understanding of the universe.

Among the spiritual states most frequently described in literature is the so-called "cosmic consciousness." This is a state in which the person witnesses his own actions as if watching someone else act. He is not overjoyed when his actions succeed, nor is he depressed if they don't. He will usually see the finer or subtler bodies of people and objects and the interactions between people as energy flows between them. In other words, he will see people acting simultaneously on the different levels of consciousness. An all-pervading peace settles on him as he understands that he is an immortal spirit, operating on this level to gain experience. He understands the hints that Nature gives him in symbolic form, which say: "Here, look, this is how I operate." He understands the meaning of "as above, so below" and knows that Nature will tend to reuse a successful design many times over, on all levels of creation, with perhaps slight modifications. In short, the design of the microcosm reflects the structure of the macrocosm, and vice versa.

There are states above that of cosmic consciousness. Those are states in which Nature opens up to the observer and shows its underlying principles and structure. In this state, a person can know anything that is happening in the cosmos in an instant. He is not bound by space or time.

Indeed, communication in the cosmos does not depend on time, as we hope to show later.*

Perhaps you're asking, at this point, "Well, but who is running the show? Who is demonstrating all these purportedly wondrous things to the people in high spiritual states?" The answer is that it is the "higher self." This higher self is the highest component of man and is a chip off the old block. It is a small part or an element of the Creator.

We understand the difficulties some people may have with the concept of a Creator. However, we find greater difficulties in assuming that there is no one responsible for the creation of the cosmos. Since no one will argue or try to deny the existence of the physical universe, we find it much more natural to assume that there is someone who *is* minding the store. It would be difficult to prove the opposite.

The higher self is.the "spirit within us," and being part of the Creator, the higher selves are all connected and communicating with each other. It is the business of the higher self to put the personality through the experiences of life and interactions with others, thereby gaining knowledge and learning to know itself. In a way, we may say now that the whole universe is an information-gathering system. The Creator breaks himself up into little units in order to be able to experience all the possible interactions among his particles on all possible levels, thereby learning to know himself. Evolution is the built-in urge that pushes all matter to higher and higher complexity, allowing experiences to occur at ever-higher levels.

The higher self cannot effectively interact with a physical body that has not been properly developed. It communi-

* It is interesting to mention in this context a survey conducted on the U.S. population in 1975, in which people were asked whether they have had any mystical experiences. Forty percent answered positively. One of the common features of these experiences, according to the survey, was that "time has come to a stop." By now, after reading Chapter 4, the reader should be in a position to explain this unusual phenomenon. This survey was the work of Andrew M. Greeley and William C. McReady of the University of Chicago, National Opinion Research Center. Available from: Sage Publications, Inc., Beverly Hills, California.

cates, therefore, with the psyche or the soul. It takes many lifetimes and a sustained effort to develop one's consciousness to a point at which direct interaction between the personality and the higher self becomes possible. However, once that point has been reached, the person becomes guided directly by the higher self. He starts relying more and more on intuitive knowledge, which is funneled to him directly from the highest possible source. At first he intuits, and later he knows this source. It makes him happy and content to feel that his experiences on this high level are a contribution to the total experience bank of the universe.

Summary

Meaningful breakthroughs in science come through intuitive leaps.

The material presented here is self-validating because with some effort these statements can be checked out by anyone. This will be a subjective validation.

The time has come to utilize knowledge that is gained by subjective means. The "observer" is our sensing, feeling, information-processing apparatus. It serves as a bridge between the material body and the spirit. The "observer" is the psyche or the soul.

Intuitive knowledge comes in chunks and is processed later.

The higher self is the spiritual *us*. It communicates to us through the soul or psyche because it cannot effectively interact with a material body. All higher selves are connected and are in constant communication.

8. A MODEL OF THE UNIVERSE

We have arrived at a point at which we should start putting all the ideas mentioned before into a consistent framework or "model of the universe." We have to show how instant communication is possible in our universe; we have to show that all knowledge is already here and available; we have to show how all the different levels of consciousness fit into our proposed model of the universe; and last but not least, we should be able to show that within our present physical universe we can find structures corresponding to our model, which would justify the rule postulated earlier, "as above, so below." In other words, we should be able to see somewhere within our visible universe a physical structure that would be a small-scale model of the larger universe we are postulating.

First, let us look at the model of the universe currently in favor in the scientific community. It is the Friedmann-Gamov general astrophysical model of the "big bang" universe.

The big bang

This is how it works: At some time, long ago, all matter in the universe was located in one compact, very hot ball having an enormous density. It was a kind of cosmic egg with all matter and space contained in it. There existed nothing but this primeval fireball. Then somehow this egg got the urge to expand or explode, and did so. This explosion, the "big bang," was supposed to have been everywhere concentric and uniform, which means that matter together with space started expanding evenly in all directions.

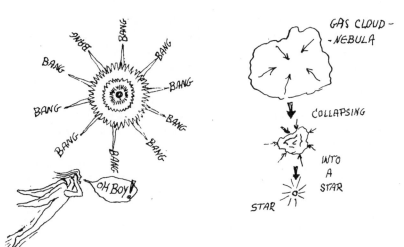

At first, matter was in the form of very high-temperature, high-frequency radiation and, as it expanded, it eventually cooled to a point at which larger stable components of matter began to appear. These were the first elementary particles of our familiar solid matter: the neutrons, the electrons, and the protons. Later, the simple elements were formed out of this soup of hot primordial particles. Hydrogen and helium atoms were formed. These produced huge clouds, or nebulae, which started breaking up into smaller units. These, in turn, started condensing due to their own gravitational pull, thus forming the basis for the evolving galaxies. The clouds of matter within these nebulae became more and more compact, which caused a rise in temperature of their centers.

The first protostars appeared in the form of blobs of glowing hydrogen gas. In time, very high temperatures were reached inside their cores. These temperatures kept rising until nuclear reactions were eventually achieved. The nuclear reactions produced much heat and light; thus, the first heavenly bodies, similar to our sun, were born. In the core of these stars, heavier elements were being cooked, and eventually a variety of elements that make up our present physical bodies were synthesized in the stars. It should make us proud to know that the elements composing our bodies were made in these great radiant stars.

Another aspect of the big-bang theory is the assumption that since the time of the big-bang explosion all matter has been distributed as if on the surface of an ever-expanding balloon.* This surface is growing, and therefore all islands of matter that we call galaxies have ever since been running away from each other. We can see it happening today when we look at the distant galaxies. All the distant galaxies that we see through our telescopes are running away from our Milky Way galaxy and from each other.

It means that the volume of our universe is constantly increasing, and this is why we call it the "expanding universe." Whether this expanding universe eventually reverses itself, starts collapsing, and ends up as it was before — one big, glowing, hot blob of matter — has not yet been decided by the scientists.

Naturally, the idea of such a pulsating universe would be aesthetically more satisfying than a one-shot universe. All the processes in the universe seem to be cyclic, and it would be most unlikely that the largest process of them all would not be so. The smaller process should mirror the large one — this, at least, is our belief.

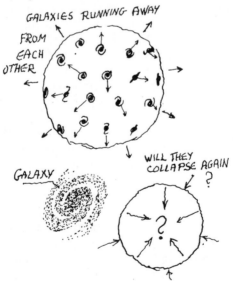

* It is actually distributed on the hypersurface of a hyper-balloon.

The continuous big-bang universe

One of the obvious results of a concentric and uniform big bang, as we have described it, would be homogeneity and isotropy* of the expanding universe. However, some measurements seem to show a bit of anisotropy, or unevenness, involved in the expanding universe. This is possibly suggested by the distribution of the so-called quasars (quasistellar objects).

Quasars are very distant and unusual galaxies. They are compact and starlike, emitting tremendous amounts of energy in radio waves and visible light. There are as yet no sufficient explanations for the amount of energy emitted by the quasars. (They emit about a thousand times as much energy as a regular galaxy and behave in other unusual ways.) They fluctuate greatly in brightness within a few days and in general are misbehaving and enigmatic "objects."

Sometimes, when such a quasar happens to be disposed to us at the right angle, we can see in its portrait an unusual feature (Photo of Quasar 3C273. Plate 1.): a luminous jet of matter issuing from its center (Fig. 37). This jet clearly is a beam of matter ejected from the center of the quasar due to some pressure buildup inside it. What we see here is an explosion of a different kind from that of the big bang. It is a controlled, nonconcentric explosion. Let us try to visualize what is happening here.

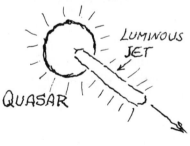

Fig. 37   **Plate 1**

* Isotropy means sameness in all directions.

Suppose we have a ball of very hot, dense matter floating in space. It stands to reason that due to energy radiation from its surface, the outside surface or skin of this ball will be cooler than its center and therefore possibly more "viscous." Let us suppose that the pressure inside this ball grows to a point at which it is about to explode. The chances are that the surface of the ball will always have a weak point at some place, and as the pressure grows, it is this weak spot that will sooner or later burst and allow a jet of matter to squirt out. As this happens, an equilibrium will eventually be set up between the pressure buildup inside the sphere and the amount of matter that escapes through the hole in the skin. What we have now is a situation similar to that of a rubber balloon filled with air and pricked with a needle. The air will escape, and the balloon will slowly deflate.

If we take this model and say, "Well, why couldn't we have the big original cosmic egg behave this way?" the answer is that it may very well have done just that. Let us consider one more clue that reinforces our assumption of a more viscous skin of the surface of this original body. It is that no counterjet is visible on the opposing side of the quasar (See Plate 1). We know that the reaction to a mass being ejected from one side of such a body will tend to cause a counterjet of equal size to appear on the other side of it. However, this is not the case in the observed quasars. The counterjet is not visible because its energy may have been absorbed by the more viscous and "elastic" surface of this body on the side opposite to the jet.

The idea that nuclei of galaxies are chips off the old block is not new; it has been mentioned lately by the Russian astronomer Ambartsumian, who in the past has been shown to have had very good intuitive insights concerning matters that, in spite of general disbelief, were later found to be correct.* He suggests that the nuclei of galaxies existed from the very beginning, possibly as fragments remaining from the original big bang, and we shall use this line of thought to develop our model of the universe.

* Oort, J. "Galaxies and the Universe." *Science*, Vol. 170, December 25, 1970, p. 1369.

The hatching or the cosmic egg

We shall start again with a ball of highly compressed matter or radiation floating in empty space, which we will call the core or nucleus. This space is not a component of our usual "space-time," rather a space that serves as a stage for the unfolding of space-time as we know it. We shall call it "protospace" or ground substance. Then for some reason this ball of matter gets the urge to expand or explode. Let us utilize the analogy of the quasar jet for the big bang. It will be a bang but not quite as big a bang as Gamov's. This bang will cause a jet of matter to emerge on one side of our egg. We have to assume that this jet is moving with a velocity that is below the escape velocity for this system, so that after leaving the nucleus, the jet of matter will now undergo the same processes as we described before for the big bang. There will be a cooling of the radiation, elementary particles will start to form, clouds of hydrogen and helium will condense into stars, and these stars will eventually die — either explode or degenerate, thus spewing heavier elements in the form of cosmic dust into space. These, in turn, will become new stars, etc., etc. The jet will also expand as it moves away from the source and will start to slow down due to the gravitational pull of the core. This is Phase I in our sketch (Fig. 38).

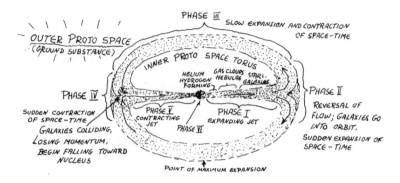

Fig. 38

Sooner or later the jet will slow down completely, expand into a mushroom shape, and start falling back toward its source. This is Phase II. It will do so because of the gravitational attraction of the enormous mass of the nucleus. This action is analogous to the behavior of a jet of water leaving the nozzle of a fountain that is pointed in a vertical direction away from the ground. We can indeed look at this flow of matter as though it were a somewhat viscous fluid.*

Now comes Phase III, the trip back to the source. This curved envelope of matter is clearly going to miss the nucleus due to its inertia, overshooting it and then slowing down again due to the gravitational pull of the core. Eventually, it will flow back toward the center; this is Phase IV. Then the two fronts of matter of opposing velocity will collide, lose momentum, and fall in toward the nucleus in a narrowing jet. This is Phase V. It is important to realize that the body shown in Figure 38 is actually a three-dimensional body.

---

* It should be mentioned that we look at this flow as though all matter in space-time behaves like viscous fluid. It can be considered as such because on the time scale of our large model the life span of stars and other "solid" matter is very short. They just blink into existence and blink out. They go from "dust to dust," so to speak. Such dust will be bound by intergalactic magnetic and gravitational fields into a medium that behaves as a viscous fluid. Thus, the universe is not "chunky" on a large time scale.

Such a body can be visualized as an elongated donut with a long thin hole through its center. This hollow ovoid shape is called a torus. We have here a torus which is constantly turning itself inside out, with matter flowing into the center core, through it, and out, thus forming the outgoing jet. This is analogous to a rotating smoke ring.

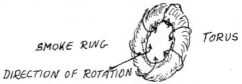

SMOKE RING   TORUS

DIRECTION OF ROTATION

However, our model of the universe is a flattened form of that smoke ring, having a much smaller hole through it. In order to visualize the inner torus, it may be useful at this point to use a kitchen variety of our model of the universe. It may serve as a good analogy. In Figure 39, we can see the metamorphosis of an unbaked jelly donut in the shape of the universe. As starting conditions, we have to assume that the jelly is distributed inside the donut as an even ring of fixed thickness and that the dough is still pliable. If we put now a thin, round stick inside this donut and start patting the dough around the stick until it assumes the required ovoid form, we shall observe that the inside jelly ring stretches out into an elongated ring. This inner jelly torus represents our protospace trapped inside the space-time envelope of the torus of our universe. If we can visualize the jelly being outside the donut as well as inside it, then we have the correct picture of this model; since the jelly is what we call protospace, or ground substance, it is the original space that later, when matter appeared, became spacetime.

METAMORPHOSIS OF A JELLY DONUT INTO A MODEL OF THE UNIVERSE

(IN FOUR SIMPLE STEPS)

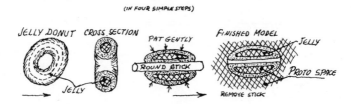

JELLY DONUT   CROSS SECTION   PAT GENTLY   FINISHED MODEL   JELLY

                                 ROUND STICK   PROTO SPACE

        JELLY   REMOVE STICK

Fig. 39

When in Phase IV the outer envelope converges upon itself, it will tend to converge to a single point. The density of galaxies at such a point or volume would be very high and cause many collisions between galaxies traveling in opposite directions. As a result, these galaxies will lose their opposing velocity components due to these collisions, slow down, and eventually start falling toward the nucleus.

Now comes Phase VI. As matter continues to fall toward the nucleus, it becomes denser, and by the time it reaches the nucleus, the gravitational collapse ensues. Gravitational collapse is a situation in which matter cannot resist the gravitational forces any longer and becomes compressed to such a degree that its density can be measured in tons per cubic inch. When matter becomes so dense, its gravitational attraction becomes so strong that it will pull back the light that is given off by this process of rapid collapse (Fig. 40A). Such a state of matter is called a "black hole" because light that could come and tell the story of this catastrophe cannot escape the fate of the rest of the matter and is sucked down into the funnel from which there is no escape. This funnel is shaped by the curvature of the space-time, which becomes very steep as the density of matter increases.

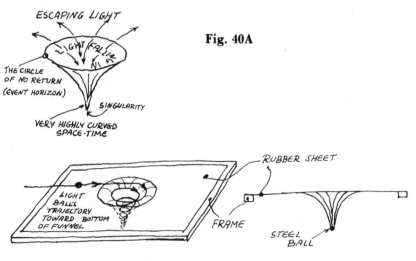

ESCAPING LIGHT

LIGHT FALLING

THE CIRCLE OF NO RETURN (EVENT HORIZON)

SINGULARITY

VERY HIGHLY CURVED SPACE-TIME

Fig. 40A

LIGHT BALL'S TRAJECTORY TOWARD BOTTOM OF FUNNEL

FRAME

RUBBER SHEET

STEEL BALL

Fig. 40B   **Fig. 40C**

A two-dimensional analogy of space-time will serve us here to elucidate this matter of curvature of space-time. Suppose we have a sheet of thin rubber stretched over a frame (Fig. 40B.). This is space-time with no big chunks of matter in it. Suppose now that we locate a big mass such as a star in this frame. We will represent this star by a heavy steel ball. The steel ball is going to stretch the rubber sheet and sink into a deep, funnel-like depression (Fig. 40C). This funnel-like depression represents the bending of space-time about a heavy object. We may say that gravitational pull arises as a result of the bending of space-time. That can be seen by simply rolling a light ball toward the funnel-like depression produced by the "star." The trajectory of the light ball will be deflected from the straight line; it will spiral and fall into the funnel to join the "star" (Fig. 40B). It will act as if it were "attracted by the 'star'." The denser and the heavier the object, the sharper the curvature of this funnel. For very dense objects, the bottom of the funnel becomes very stretched out until it becomes a small point.

It seems that there is no hope for matter that has fallen into the black hole. The denser it becomes, the larger the crushing forces on it; and the larger the crushing forces, the denser matter becomes. In short, matter is crushing itself out of existence. But since matter is energy, where does the energy go? According to our physicists, it goes through a singularity point, a point theoretically of zero size that is the bane of mathematicians and physicists because laws of Nature break down in the singularity state. Having gone through this point, it reappears in a "different universe." It would appear there as an upwelling of energy that would fit a description of a "white hole," the opposite of a black hole. This white hole is a nucleus or source from which matter is emerging; in fact, it is like that "cosmic egg" described at the beginning of this chapter.

We now have an appreciation of the general qualities of the black and white holes; thus armed, we can conclude that the initial cosmic egg white hole must have come from a black hole because when all the matter in the universe is condensed in one spot, a gravitational collapse must ensue and matter will collapse to a singularity, as we have mentioned before.

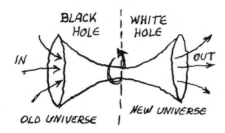

Fig. 41

Our universe, then, has emerged from a white hole, which happened to be the output end of a black hole, and we are proposing that the universe is undergoing a continuous process of death and rebirth. Matter that issues from the white hole appears to us as the "cosmic egg" or the primordial fireball of the big-bang theory. This matter has fallen into a black hole in the "past" universe. Black hole and white hole, then, are "back to back." One is the input end and the final repository of all matter that has gone through one evolutionary cycle, and the other side, the white hole, is the source of all matter, which reappears in the "new" universe. As matter goes through the death-birth pangs of the black-white holes, it re-emerges thoroughly homogenized and re-energized for a new trip through the evolutionary cycle.

According to John T. Taylor,* things are not as bad for matter that falls into a *rotating* black hole (also called Kerr black hole) (Fig. 41). Here matter doesn't go through a point of zero size; rather, the singularity looks like a ring, and as the black hole becomes a narrow funnel on the input side, there is a symmetrical funnel attached to it at the output side, where matter emerges. We know that in this present universe everything is rotating, from electrons to galaxies; the rotating black-white holes could just be the source of all that rotary motion in our universe.

It is clear now to the observant reader that once we have a black hole, there must be a white hole associated with it. They always have to come in pairs, since matter that has disappeared in the black hole has to reappear somewhere. Such

* Taylor, John, *Black Holes: The End of the Universe?* New York: Random House, 1973; London: Souvenir Press, 1973.

a pair is what we shall refer to as the nucleus. The nucleus is Phase VI in our sketch in Figure 38 and is the beginning and the end of "time" in our universe. We can take the birth of our matter that occurs in the nucleus as a reference date. There it is that "time" of this universe starts. From there on we can measure the processes of the development of matter as described before, from radiation to atoms and galaxies, either in terms of time or of distance traveled by the jet of matter emitted by the nucleus (Fig. 42). Thus, "time" becomes just a measure of distance, a dimension overlapping one of the three dimensions of our space.

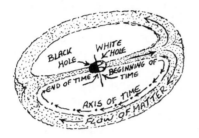

Fig. 42

The length of "time" needed to go once around this torus is all the "time" there is in this universe. Because if we go through such a cycle and fall into the black hole, then re-emerge from the white hole, we have emerged into a new universe again. So time is not flowing anywhere; it just is. It is *matter* that moves along, not time. As we move in space, we are also moving along the time axis. If we could stop our movement in space entirely, it is possible that we should experience no passage of time at all.

Figure 43 shows a point source out of which matter emerges in an expanding jet, which constitutes our "expanding universe." We can visualize only a small part of this, so we are going to call it the "observable universe." This is the volume limited by the reach of our telescopes. It is just a small bubble within the enormous structure. Suppose now that we position ourselves somehow outside the universe. We would then see the walls of our bubble expanding as the volume of the jet increases. If we take a small bubble of space at A (Fig. 43), we find that its volume has increased as it moved toward point B, and as we watch the same bubble move to point C, there is clearly more expansion there. So our space-time is expanding, and the rate of expansion is the greatest at the point at which the flow of matter reverses direction, that is, in the funnel area of Phase II. This is how the observed unevenness in the distribution of matter in the universe may come about. If the bubble of our observable universe is close to the entrance into the funnel, it may suffer an uneven expansion, which would then account for the observed differences in the velocity of galaxies and quasars in the sky. We shall return to this later. Thus, we have seen matter and space-time go through phases of expansion and contraction.

Matter that flows out of the nucleus located in the center of the torus sooner or later finds itself on the outside of the torus as it goes about its stages of evolution. Afterward, beyond Phase III, space-time will start contracting and eventually collapsing back into the nucleus. That would constitute one evolutionary cycle of this universe. Matter that falls into the nucleus will re-emerge into a "new" universe, as we have shown before. Thus, we have a constant flow of matter moving through the nucleus. From the standpoint of matter that has gone through the nucleus and emerged from the white hole, this is a brand-new universe; but for us observers, watching from outside, it is just the other side of the same old universe. All that happened was that matter got squeezed, homogenized, turned into *radiation* — and it's ready for another run.

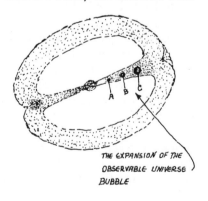

THE EXPANSION OF THE
OBSERVABLE UNIVERSE
BUBBLE   **Fig. 43**

Fig. 44

Suppose now that we, the outside observers, somehow arrived on the scene before this universe was created. All we could then see would be darkness (as the good old Bible says) because even if all the matter of which the universe is made were present, we could not see it because it would be in a black-hole state with no matter flowing into it or out of it, and space-time would be curled up tightly around it. All we could see in the endless darkness would be some more darkness. In short, we could never see a *potential* universe; we could see only one that started acting — i.e. we would be able to see only a universe in the process of creation. By creation we mean the eruption of matter from the white-hole side of the nucleus (Fig. 44).

Let us contemplate for a moment the boundless dark space we are in as we are about to witness the act of creation or the unfolding or our familiar space-time torus. We are floating in a space in which there is *no time* because there is *no motion*. Matter introduces motion and with it time. This space is the stage within which creation is taking place; it is the unchanging, eternal, immutable background from which all creation arises. This may sound familiar to you if you remember Chapter 5. It sounds as though this space, which we have called protospace, fits closely our lengthy description of the absolute. It has all the needed characteristics used to describe the absolute. Are the two identical? Or is this protospace only one component of the absolute?

Of light and life

Consider now what happens to light under these conditions. When the jet of radiating matter (matter is at first in the form of radiation) is ejected from the nucleus, it will propagate into protospace and thus *create* space-time. This space-time will be *bent* by the large mass of the jet and thus force the photons to follow it in an envelope *surrounding* the jet.

Figure 40B shows how a ball or, in our case, a photon will be trapped by the curvature of space-time. If we visualize the white hole as being located at the bottom of the funnel, as shown in Figure 40B, and the jet of matter extending vertically upward, then the light emitted by the jet will be confined to circulate within this funnel.

Light will thus follow the curvature of space-time caused by the mass of the jet and will therefore not be able to penetrate into the space between the central jet and the return flow envelope of the universe. (See Fig. 45). A torus of protospace is thus trapped within the envelope of matter. Remember, this is still a piece of the original protospace. It is the jelly in the donut. Light is thus confined to move more or less closely along with matter. Observers located in the jet portion cannot see the light emitted by the outer envelope across the trapped protospace; they can see only along the path of matter. Light emitted by the jet or the envelope will eventually turn back on itself (Fig. 45).

We may ask now, at what point down the jet did life, as we know it, begin? The reader is aware that life on the physical level is not the only form of life there is. In fact, it is one of the latest forms of life to appear. Consciousness, as you may

Fig. 45

remember, is the underlying structure of matter and life; it has therefore also been the underlying principle of the black hole-white hole nucleus. As matter became more and more complex, consciousness began to manifest in the physical realities, in life forms known to us. However, consciousness, intelligence, and life were always tied together and always present everywhere.

There are some indications on the position of our "observable universe" within this big structure. By observable universe we do not mean only the universe as limited by the range of our radio or optical telescopes. There is, however, an absolute limit to our horizon, and that is the horizon of the velocity of light. We know that all galaxies are running away from us at speeds proportional to their distance from us. In other words, the larger the distance, the faster the galaxies are running away. When the farthest galaxies approach the speed of light, they will simply disappear from our sight, simply because light, having a fixed velocity of about 186,000 miles per second, will not be able to reach us since the source of light is moving away from us with a speed approaching that of the light coming in our direction. If the hypothetical galaxy will be running away from us at, say, 1,900,000 miles per second, its light can never reach us. It is therefore our absolute visual horizon. To our present knowledge that absolute horizon lies at a distance of about 10 billion light-years. The observable universe, then, will constitute an expanding bubble of about 20 billion light-years in circumference, floating around somewhere in this much larger structure.

Our position in the flow

It is possible to determine the approximate position of our galaxy within this torus-shaped universe by extrapolating from the uneven distribution of galaxies as known to us today. That is, as we look out of our galaxy into space, we find that other galaxies are not running away from us at an even clip, thereby distorting the otherwise theoretically perfect sphere of the expanding universe. The data are changing all the time, but it seems that our skies are divided into two general areas, one centering about the northern pole of our galaxy, the other area being approximately opposite to it, or about 30 degrees away from the southern pole of our galaxy. The galaxies in the northern portion seem to be running away from us faster than the ones in the southern portion of the galaxy.* This also indicates that those galaxies are also more distant from us than their southern counterparts. This effect is observed most obviously in the case of the quasars, the most distant objects we can see. They form, according to Burbidge and Burbidge, two fairly clearly defined regions in the northern and southern portions of the galaxy.† The northern group is spread out over a large circle about the pole, while the southern group of quasars is bunched more tightly.

This would indicate that our observable universe bubble is stretched into a kidney shape, its northern portion bulging and expanding faster than the southern. This is because space-time is expanding much more rapidly in the funnel area. The little arrows drawn in the bubble show the relative rate of expansion, and the position of our galaxy is marked within the bubble (Fig. 46). This is, of course, not drawn to scale; our galaxy would be just a very small speck within the bubble, and so would the bubble in proportion to the rest of the universe.

Suppose now that the average level of civilization of our galaxy is that represented by our planet. We would certainly expect that life on galaxies older than ours — that is, those further down the line of evolution — would be much more evolved. Galaxies that are reaching the peak of the expansion of our space-time (this occurs halfway down the outer envelope of the torus) would be on an even higher level of

---

* Rubin et al. "A Curious Distribution of Radial Velocities of ScI Galaxies." *The Astrophysical Journal.* 1973. Vol. 183, L111-L115.

† Burbidge, Geoffrey and Margaret. *Quasi-Stellar Objects.* San Francisco, Cal.: Freeman, 1967; Reading: W.H. Freeman, 1968. These data have been superseded by newer data indicating that there is an even distribution of quasars across the universe. However, still newer data show an uneven distribution of velocities.

evolution. I am making a parallel here between the expansion or volume of spacetime and the "expansion" of consciousness. Beyond this peak we can therefore expect a slow decline in the general level of consciousness, which will degenerate rapidly as the galaxies draw nearer to their ultimate destiny in the black hole.

We can be sure that we are sharing a universe in which all the problems that may seem to be problems to us at present have been solved over and over by civilizations ahead of us in "time." We may say, therefore, that all knowledge that was ever generated is potentially available to us at some point or other in our universe.

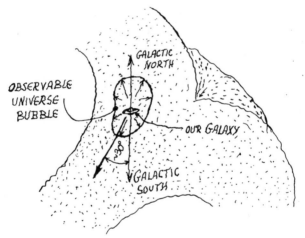

Fig. 46

Summary

We have described the big bang, a concentric expansion of the universe, and the development of galaxies and stars. Our continuous big-bang model of the universe is patterned after the jet-emitting quasar. In our model, the jet slows down, expands, and turns back upon itself, eventually forming an ovoid shape. This ovoid shape has a nucleus in its center, which is a black hole-white hole object. It is the source of all matter in the universe and its final repository.

"Time" is seen as the distance covered by matter emitted from the white-hole side of the nucleus, going around the shell of the torus, until it enters the black hole.

Our "observable universe" is a tiny bubble within the torus of the universe.

The position of our galaxy can be located by taking into account the anisotropies in the distribution of distant galaxies.

The general expansion of consciousness is linked to the expansion on the torus of the universe.

9. THE "HOW TO" OF INTUITIVE KNOWLEDGE

"Knowledge is structured in consciousness."
— Maharishi Mahesh Yogi
quoting the *Vedas*.

We came to the conclusion in the last chapter that all knowledge that was ever generated is at present available in our galaxy and in the more advanced ones. These galaxies would be further down the road from us toward the largest diameter of the outer envelope of our universe. Naturally, the question arises: Is there any way to tap this knowledge? The answer is yes.

Let us go back to Chapter 4, where we described the experiment with time. We were talking there about the "observer," a nonmaterial entity expanding at practically infinite speeds into space at the point of rest of the pendulum or body. This "observer" is the nonphysical "us," our psyche. It contains all the information, all the knowledge which we collected during our lifetimes. It also contains our personalities, our intellects, and our intuitions. This package moves for a very short period of time in a spacelike dimension (Fig. 47) to fill all space. Then it returns, as if nothing had happened, into the body in order to run it again.

We can visualize this by imagining ourselves to be collapsed balloons, which are inflated instantly to a very large diameter, then collapse just as instantly. Every living thing, including entities on other planets in our galaxy or outside our galaxy, undergoes this pulsation.

There are some theoretical problems here; therefore, before we go any further, we have to make two important assumptions: (1) that the information — that is, the "observer" — behaves in a coherent fashion as it expands; and (2) that the information can move at velocities faster than light.

First, coherency is important because we have to show that the information forms interference patterns in space-time or protospace as it expands. You may remember from our description of the hologram in Chapter 1 what an interference pattern is. We know that holograms can be made only with coherent light, and we know that holograms or interference patterns contain in each element of their surface or volume *all* the information about the whole system, just as the chromosomes in each cell of our body contain all the information about how to build another copy of our bodies. We know, of course, that in practice it is the sperm and the egg cells that specialize in the business of making copies of us human beings, but in principle all cells contain all the information about us. So as we, the "observers," rapidly expand in the spacelike dimension, we form interference patterns with other "observers" as they, too, expand, and our information interacts with the information from these other "observers." This all happens against the background of the reference frequency or the absolute. To go back to the hologram, our "observers" are the "working beam," while the absolute is the reference, the "inexperienced, naive beam."

Second, the theory of relativity states that information cannot travel faster than the velocity of light. I hope that

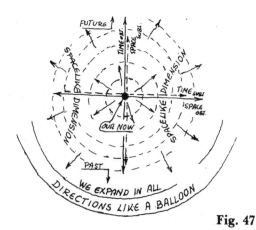

Fig. 47

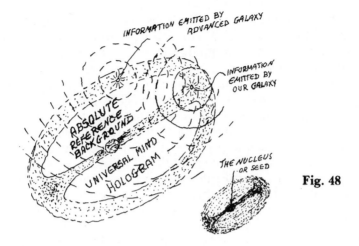

Fig. 48

this will eventually be shown not to be the case as ways are found to get around these limitations. Workers in the field of faster-than-light particles (tachyons)* are presently grappling with these problems. As a result, a more encompassing theory is emerging that will allow information to tunnel through into a spacelike dimension and propagate there in a coherent fashion. Let us see now what our model of the universe will look like in the light of the things just discussed.

Figure 48 shows what happens to our "observers" as we radiate out into space. Our wave fronts are shown crossing the whole length of the inner torus of the universe, and so are the "observers" ejected from advanced galaxies. In the outer envelope of the universe, these "observer" wave fronts are shown now interacting, just as did the wave fronts produced by the pebbles we dropped into the pan in the description of the hologram in Chapter 1. From that description we know that not only can we read the information from every unit area of the pan, but we can also trace each bit of information to its source. Thus, as our "observers," or information waves, are periodically expanding into the inner torus

* Bilaniuk, Olexa-Myron, and Sudarshan, George. "Particles Beyond the Light Barrier," *Physics Today*, 1969, pp. 43-51.

of the universe, so are the "observers," or information waves, of everybody else. For a tiny fraction of a second we form an information hologram with them, and this is repeated many times a second. The reference frequency against which all this interaction occurs is the absolute. Since all information that has been generated in this universe appears there, we can call that area the "universal mind" (Fig. 48). People having "intuitive insights" get solutions from there, and people with high levels of consciousness, who are able to extend their subjective time, can learn and bring back useful information about the goings-on in the "universal mind." This communication appears to one as simply "knowing." Such a person just seems to know things that other people usually don't know. This knowledge is often about the coming events, details of people's lives to which the "knower" has no access, or knowledge of who is on the line before the telephone rings, etc. These things fall under the heading of clairvoyance, clairaudience, etc. There are higher and lower levels of development of these faculties. On the higher levels, information can be obtained about the nature of the universe and the cosmos, depending where the interests of the particular person lie.

These faculties arise either spontaneously or can be cultivated. When we deal with human affairs in objective time, information arises within the field of the planet; it is "local" information. We would therefore expect little or no time lag in its transfer, whether we use telepathy or an intercontinental phone call. Personally, I would rely more on information transmitted over the phone. The advantages of telepathy or clairvoyance become evident, however, when trying to obtain information about other systems such as distant stars, as astronomers do. Such a system of communication with no time lag would be revolutionary because what the astronomers observe through their instruments is the past, sometimes counted in billions of years. That is, it takes that long for information coming from a neighboring star to reach us, because the average distance between stars is about four to five light-years. They may be looking at objects no longer in existence.

We know that the Andromeda galaxy is at a distance of

about two million light-years from us, that is, it takes light
this much time to travel this distance. If the Andromeda
galaxy exploded yesterday, we would not know of this event
for at least two million years. However, in our model we are
showing that by extending one's subjective time, one can
obtain information from Andromeda without having to
wait four million years for a return signal. The information
transfer is instant, both for the people on Andromeda and
on Earth, provided they go to the trouble of learning how to
raise their level of consciousness. *Indeed, the whole universe
is in constant and instant communication.* Any serious
event can be known across the universe instantly by consciousnesses whose interest or business it is to know these
things.

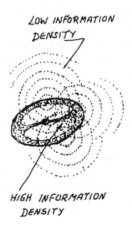

LOW INFORMATION
DENSITY

HIGH INFORMATION
DENSITY

We have seen that the expansion of the observers has no
limits because they move in a spacelike dimension at almost
infinite velocity and therefore expand toward the center of
the universe as much as toward the outside. Thus, the information will be available to anyone outside our universe.
However, the information density will be greatest toward
the center of our universe and with it the clarity of vision.
This is because information waves, that is, "observers,"
emitted from all points on the shell will tend to be more con-
centrated toward the central axis of the torus. Information

generated by us and leaving the universe will weaken rapidly and disperse in the vast protospace outside our universe.

Here is where the "quality of consciousness," which we have defined by "frequency response," comes into play. We said in Chapter 5 that frequency response may be described by the "agility" or speed with which a given system responds to a stimulus. We shall now take as the "stimulus" the very short period of time allowed us by the period of time to expand into space and to collapse back. The higher a person's level of consciousness, the higher his frequency response; the higher his frequency response, the farther away from his point of origin his observer can penetrate. We also know that the higher one's level of consciousness, the larger his $\updownarrow$ angle, which means that he can expand into space with a higher velocity, and have more subjective time available for observation. In short, a person or "observer" with a higher level of consciousness will fill space farther and faster than one who is not so developed.

It is known from optics of holograms that although all the elements of the hologram contain complete information about the objects portrayed in the hologram, if we illuminate just a small area of the hologram, the image will appear fuzzy — that is, it will have a low definition; while if we illuminate a large area of the same hologram, the image will appear much sharper. Therefore, persons with higher levels of consciousness will see past or future events more sharply than those occupying lower levels of consciousness.

The modular universe

When talking about communication on this level, we have to take into account other consciousnesses, not just the human kind, that abound in our universe. As we mentioned before, we human beings are units of consciousness that make up a larger consciousness, and a group of these larger consciousnesses makes up an even larger unit of consciousness, and so on. In short, both the material and the nonmaterial universes are modular. Just as the basic unit for the physical universe, the atom, is repeated many times to build larger and larger hierarchies, so are consciousnesses built up to form larger consciousnesses. A group of atoms makes up a molecule, that is, the hierarchy above the atom. A group of these makes up a piece of matter, let us say a crystal, visible to the naked eye, or makes up a simple living creature, which will be a hierarchy above that of the crystal. The further we go up the hierarchies, the less the structure of that hierarchy resembles the properties of the original physical building block, the atom. Only after many, many hierarchies will the structure of the original building block, the atom, be repeated again. In this case, it will appear to a certain degree to be reflected in the solar system. An elliptical galaxy will even more closely represent a simple atom in shape.

The shape of our model of the universe and the flow of matter in it resemble very much the shape of the electrical fields around a seed or an egg. The seed represents unique behavior, and this is why I chose it as representative of the universe in its actions. Let us take a tree as an example. The seed is potentially located everywhere in the tree. Eventually, the four-dimensional (time-space) matrix of the tree is condensed into the seed. The vibrating molecules of the genes carrying the information about the form of the tree have somehow coded the *spatial and temporal* form of the tree, so that we can say that the seed carries not only the information about the *shape* of the tree but also its *unfoldment in time,* or the sequence of the different stages in its growth and their timing. The spatial coding is given by the amino-acid sequence; the temporal coding may possibly be given by the relationship of the frequencies of vibration of the molecular segments with respect to each other.

The seed is a unique structure because in it space-time has been condensed and stored, awaiting the proper objective time for its unfoldment. Therefore, it is the representation of the tree in an *altered and higher state of consciousness.* It is a tree that has moved into its subjective space-time, in which time and space have lost their ordinary meaning. It is a state in which "time has stopped" as far as the tree is concerned. The outer objective manifestation of this state of the tree is the seed. Later, when the objective conditions become favorable, the tree will come out of its *meditative, hybernating* state as a seed and unfold in objective space-time as a mature tree. The seed, in other words, is a more basic structure than the tree because in its qualities it is closer to the absolute.

Here we might be able to shed some light on the "Which came first, the chicken or the egg?" controversy. If the egg feels lonely and wants company, the only way for it to have more eggs around is to go through the nuisance of becoming a chicken, which eventually will lay more eggs. Of course, the advantage for the egg of being a chicken is the opportunity to interact with its environment and thus evolve to a higher level of consciousness.

We should, therefore, see in the seed-tree duality a unique function of Nature. It does not matter whether it is the seed of a tree, the egg of a chicken, a human sperm, or a seaweed egg. The seed is unique because if one could penetrate its consciousness, one would find that it "sees itself" as a full-grown tree in spite of its confinement in a tiny shell. We will expand on this further in the next chapter.

The organizing fields of life

If we take an ordinary chicken egg and very carefully make two windows, one in the top and one in the bottom of the shell, without injuring the thin membrane surrounding the contents of the egg, then, using a sensitive voltmeter with a set of silver electrodes, touch the exposed membrane at the top and the bottom of the egg (Fig. 49), we find a positive voltage at the top and a negative one at the bottom. For an unfertilized egg taken from the refrigerator, this voltage will be a steady 2.40 millivolts. When we make two more windows in the sides of the egg, facing each other, and take measurements, we find no similar potential difference. This indicates that there is an electrical field present along the long axis of the egg, which then has to turn back over itself, as shown. This behavior has been shown to be true in seaweed eggs, frog eggs, and seeds. A good account of the field around living organisms is given in *Blueprint for Immortality* by Harold Saxton Burr, professor of anatomy, at Yale

University (London: Neville Spearman, 1972). These fields seem to be penetrating and surrounding living tissue. It has also been shown that the spine of a tadpole within a frog egg lines up along the axis of this potential field in the egg. I suggest that the shape of the electrical field governing the development and the form of living beings is mirrored in the shape of our universe. Here we have another example of a form on the microscale appearing after many hierarchies of size on the macroscale. Burr calls these the *"organizing fields,"* claiming that they come first, guiding the atoms and molecules of the growing organism into its proper form. In effect, what he is saying is that an electromagnetic hologram that changes with time makes up a mold, and matter eventually fills up that mold, giving rise to a tangible body. This fits very well with the model we are developing here. It is the first work actually confirming that our matter (in this case our living bodies) is held together by a four-dimensional interference pattern.

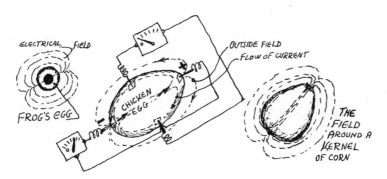

Fig. 49

We have seen in Chapter 6 that our invisible subtle bodies can be equated with "higher harmonics" of the physical body. This is a reasonably good analogy, but it gives the impression that these subtle bodies originate from the physical body. Actually, *the physical body is the end product,* so to speak, of the subtle information fields, which mold our physical body as well as all physical matter. For instance, we

know that most physical diseases are psychosomatic, or
caused by our emotional and mental components or bodies.
These bodies or fields affect the health of the physical body.
The emotional and mental bodies interpenetrate the physical body and extend into the space around it. We have seen
in Chapter 1, Figure 5, how interacting sounds could form a
physical body — a magnified crystal, in that case. We know
that the "sound" of the absolute contains very high energies. One can visualize physical matter as being a beat frequency (Chapter 1, Fig. 7C) caused by the interaction of two
such "sounds" having a slightly different frequency. Such
an interaction would cause waves of much *lower frequency
and higher amplitude*. This is, if you remember, how we
described (Chapter 5, Fig. 32) the "visible manifest aspect of
the absolute" — the physical realities.

Different kinds of beings

We have said earlier that matter contains or *is* consciousness, and now we have to draw the inevitable conclusions
from that statement: If this is the case, then our planet must
be a very large being! And the sun an even larger one. Let us
speculate for a while on such a possibility.

What happens when we lose consciousness due to some
trauma? Or when we project our psyches, as in the experiment with time? In the first case, we know that the bodies
will take care of themselves: the heart will keep on working;
breathing, though shallow, will be present; the brain will
produce its electrical output; etc. But otherwise the body
will not respond to normal sensory inputs; it will not move,
talk, or perform any of the activities that we usually associate with a waking state of consciousness. In the deep meditative state we discern similar symptoms. In both cases, our
psyches are dissociated from our bodies. In the first case,
that is, the unconscious state, consciousness wanders about
aimlessly, as if in a deep sleep state, or it may be on a
"guided tour" to other realities. In the meditative state, consciousness is separated from the body but is active on the
highest levels of creation.

We have to conclude, therefore, that the body has its own

consciousness, which is rudimentary but intelligent enough and quite capable of operating the body independently of the psyche. It is only loosely connected to the other entity, the psyche. This consciousness is the sum total of the consciousnesses of the cells of our body or the "wisdom of the inner parts," as the Bible puts it. We have here, then, two entities. One is the relatively low, rudimentary consciousness, which runs the body, and the other is the psyche, a higher-level entity, which uses the body most of the time as a focus but is independent of it. We can liken the body to an automobile. When the driver gets out and leaves the engine running, it will idle and function normally. But to give purposeful direction to the car, a driver or a higher consciousness is needed. If the consciousness running the body leaves it, the body dies.

This principle of two consciousnesses inhabiting a body can be extended to larger bodies — those of our planet, the sun, etc. We shall then have a consciousness related to the mass of the planet; it would be a rudimentary consciousness keeping the planet in running order, that is, keeping the metabolism of the planet in operation: the atmospheric circulation, ocean currents, gas balances, inner and outer temperatures, energy fields, etc. This work is being done by smaller consciousnesses that comprise the consciousness of the planet. We have described them before as Nature spirits of different sorts and sizes. The large ones delegate work to the smaller ones, and so on. The sum total of them all makes up the rudimentary consciousness of the planet.

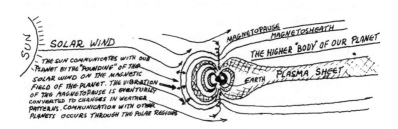

We could liken the body of the planet to that of an enormous sleeping whale whose movements are very slow except for some local shudder from time to time. On the other hand, we have the other consciousness that inhabits the planet and uses it as a temporary residence. It is an enormous consciousness, and the sum total of mankind's consciousness makes up only a fraction of this great consciousness or being. This being will guide the evolution of the human races and civilizations, will cause environmental changes to stimulate evolution in certain directions.

I suggest that an equation for the rudimentary consciousness, when developed sometime in the future, will look somehow like this:

rudimentary consciousness =
    constant x mass x flux x temperature.

The constant may be very small, somewhat like the Planck's constant. By flux I mean the amount of energy of all frequencies radiated by the mass.

The sun, having a much larger mass and temperature, will have a much larger rudimentary consciousness controlling the processes taking place in it, and it will serve as a residence for a much larger consciousness than that of the earth. The consciousness of the earth and of the other planets will be contained within the sun's consciousness and comprise a part of that being. We could call this being the higher consciousness of the sun, while the first one is the higher consciousness of our planet. These enormous intelligences are beyond our comprehension.

Consider for a moment the system we live in. Physical life is made possible by the energies supplied to us by the sun. Our bodies are made up of materials the planet is supplying. These bodies, temporarily animated, are borrowed from the planet, and then the materials used for the bodies are returned to the planet, while the psyche goes back to the reality that fits it best. That reality may be connected with that of our planet, the sun, the universe, or the cosmos, depending on its level of evolution.

We living beings play an important role in the evolution

of the rudimentary consciousness of our planet. On the whole, we are upgrading it. However, in order to live in tune with it, we have to be sensitive to its needs, the most basic of which is balance. Things that unbalance the system to a high degree cause stress in this large consciousness. By stress, in this case, we mean also emotional stress. When the imbalance becomes too great, the planet responds in its own way by natural catastrophes to return its balance.

The sun regulates life on this planet both by the amount of electromagnetic radiation, which we feel as heat and light, and by the fluctuations caused in the magnetic field of the planet: those of the ionosphere, the weather patterns, the electrostatic field of the ionosphere-earth system, and many other phenomena that until now have not been measured. The sun "talks" to the planets with its acoustical output—the solar wind.

It would take quite a bit of imagination to visualize a consciousness that runs a galaxy, a cluster of galaxies, or finally, the universe. There *is* such a consciousness, and we shall call it the Creator. All these consciousnesses are in communication with each other, and we could even eavesdrop on their conversations while in a high state of consciousness. The knowledge we would gain would be minimal since their topics of conversation are so far removed from ours.

Summary

We have a closed universe that forms an elongated hollow torus. Encased within this torus is an inner torus of protospace. Light cannot travel through the inner torus, but our psyches can.

Our psyches, which contain all our knowledge, expand periodically into that space for a very short period of time at practically infinite velocities. There the human psyches form an interference pattern with psyches of all other consciousnesses in the universe.

This interference pattern or hologram of knowledge information we can call the "universal mind." The knowledge in the universal mind is open to anyone who can extend his stay there by stretching out his subjective time while there so as to gain useful information and decipher it upon his return.

Matter contains/is consciousness. Our planet is therefore a larger consciousness, and so is the sun. A rudimentary consciousness contained in matter and in living cells maintains the life in the body. A higher consciousness, the human psyche, inhabits that body most of the time but is independent of it. The planet and the sun have also a "permanent resident" consciousness and a higher consciousness/intelligence using it as a focus or a garage.

All these consciousnesses communicate with each other and make up part of the information hologram: Communication throughout the universe is continuous and instantaneous.

Upon the "death" of the physical body, the psyche returns to its realm, finding its proper reality band with which it naturally resonates, depending on its level of evolution.

Our physical bodies are formed by organizing fields. These fields are four-dimensional electromagnetic holograms, which change in time. Our physical bodies are the end products and the result of the interactions of our subtle, nonphysical "information bodies."

10. SOME REFLECTIONS ON THE CREATOR

In Chapter 2 we looked at matter with a big microscope. The more we looked, the more we enlarged, and the less we found. We ended up with a *void*, permeated by pulsating energy fields. Even the most "solid" matter, the one that imparts most of the mass to it — the nucleus of the atom, which at first appeared as a solid grain of matter — upon a better look dissolved into a vortex of pulsating fields. Thus, we found a void to be the common denominator of all matter — its ground substance, so to speak. We human beings consider ourselves to be made up of "solid matter." However, by now we know that we are just an interference pattern of waves that is changing with time. Or, in other words, we are a four-dimensional hologram. The base for the hologram is the void that permeates and connects all creation. We have heard of this void before — that is how we have described the absolute.

As we look at the pulsating energy fields, we ask ourselves: What would happen if we should slow down the pulsation of the energy fields or stop their pulsations altogether? The answer is that we would get back our void or the absolute. It is as though the wind that has raised the ripples over the face of the sea of the absolute has stopped blowing; calm has set in, and the face of the sea is smooth again. There is no motion, therefore no time and no matter. The absolute is there, undisturbed. (Remember that this absolute is pure consciousness combined with intelligence, as mentioned in Chapter 5.)

We can see now that in order to re-establish manifest creation, we have to be able somehow to rattle or vibrate the surface of the absolute. This is no simple task, and we would not even know how to begin. But that is, of course, what Creators are for.

You may recall that the ripples on the surface of the sea of the absolute in the "fine relative" (Fig. 33A) are so small and of such a high frequency as to become invisible. The absolute is both in a state of rest and at the same time of enormous potential energy. Similarly, we have seen how infinite velocity has become a state of rest, how the birth of matter occurs simultaneously and in the same place as its death. Creation and destruction are simultaneous. Degeneration carries renewal in its core. We know that the end of time is its beginning. In short, we find that there is a level in Nature at which all extremes become reconciled and merged. It is on this level that black and white, good and evil merge into one "Is"-ness. This is also where the ultimate truth lies. The truth is not black or white; it is both. The pairs of opposites of the lower levels merge on the highest level.

We tend to view Nature through a tiny slot from a narrow angle; others see it from another angle and describe it in a different language. It sounds different, but it is not. The universe is so rich in diversity that almost anything one says about it is correct, provided one takes a broad enough view.

We have tried our hand before at designing Nature spirits; let us see now whether we can follow the actions of the Creator of a universe. We shall try to peek over His shoulder while He works. The scenario would run something like this: in the tremendous, boundless, infinite, dark void something stirs. A very great volume of the void has decided to move and is defining its boundaries. This enormous consciousness/intelligence is *separating itself from the continuum* so that it can start acting. It has thus become an individualized entity. It contains tremendous amounts of energy because the state of the absolute is a state of the highest potential energy. It is a state of rest of the pendulum.

Now the Creator has to settle down and start to draw up plans of what to do within His real estate, which is His body. He sits back in His cosmic armchair and contemplates. He realizes that unless He can produce a consciousness equal to Himself in all qualities, He may never know what He Himself is all about. So He sets out to decide on the rules of the game, that is, the laws of Nature as we know them; He invents the laws of evolution. Evolution will refine consciousness to a point at which it will resemble Him in all attributes. He will start with matter of low consciousness, make it more and more complex, and watch the emergence of the first intelligence that can contemplate itself. This would mirror one of His basic attributes and would be quite a milestone *in His development*. Let us not forget that all these processes are occurring inside Him, in His subjective time.

He will have to invent the most diverse creatures, the most diverse situations, and the most diverse events, then have His creatures go through all these possible situations and interact in all the possible ways. When all His different being will have gone through all the possible situations and interacted in all the possible ways, then He will know what He is capable of; He will then know Himself.

He uses the duality of good and evil as a catalyst to speed up the interactions: Good stands for the knowledge of His laws; and evil, for the ignorance of His ultimate laws. In other words, that which is in harmony with His laws and helps the process of evolution is "good," and that which slows it down is "evil." However, He manages to utilize both in the interest of evolution. Their constant interaction speeds up the very process of evolution.

For the more evolved creatures, free will is built into the system, so that they can eventually become co-creators. While the more simple creatures go through a present event matrix, the more evolved ones can choose from a number of possible paths. But once chosen, each path has its end result predetermined, so that it fits in with the general event matrix, while still allowing for much variety.

An event matrix can be visualized as field patterns of diverse shapes within space-time. They are embedded within the space-time in a certain sequence that best fits the evolution of consciousness. These fields either stimulate, balance, or depress certain tendencies within our psyches. When it so happens that, on its way through the expanding jet, the earth crosses a stress-producing event matrix, the result will be that certain segments of mankind—the ones most susceptible to it at the moment — will become agitated, resulting in a possible war. If the event matrix happens to be one that will produce a calming effect, then a period of peace will result. If the event matrix of war has an elongated sausage shape (Fig. 50), then as our planet crosses it the first time, we may have a war fought with clubs, while the next time around it may be fought with muskets, and the third time around A-bombs may be used. The event is the same; only technology has changed. The causes behind the war event are always the same: greed, for more wealth and territory; hatred; intolerance etc. The event sausage will have the stimulating frequencies to evoke these emotions, and as they stimulate our endocrine system, these events will tend to occur. Remember how the full moon causes the emotionally unbalanced people to commit crimes? This is a similar effect only on a grand scale. A long-event sausage may be the cause behind the saying: "History repeats itself."

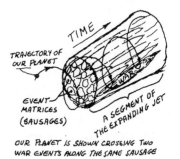

OUR PLANET IS SHOWN CROSSING TWO   **Fig. 50**
WAR EVENTS ALONG THE SAME SAUSAGE

At the beginning, the Creator watches with aloof amusement as His creatures go through the events, like a flow of animated matter. However, somewhere down the path of evolution, consciousnesses will arise that will draw His attention. These will be creatures who not only contemplate themselves but start contemplating Him. When a creature has reached a level of development at which he understands his real makeup and perceives that "Thou art That," then he becomes self-realized. The whole scheme of creation becomes transparent to him, and henceforth he will watch himself act within that scheme but at the same time remain separate from his actions. This is analogous to the way the Creator operates — acting but at the same time remaining separate and uninvolved in the action. When a creature gains this attribute of the Creator, He will appreciate it. He will set aside such a unit of consciousness and say to him: "Here, do this . . . ." It may be just doing little chores at first but sooner or later such a unit of consciousness will start guiding the evolution of other consciousnesses; that is, the being becomes a co-creator and eventually a minor god. As time goes by, more consciousnesses reach high levels, angels, humans, or nonhumans. But the goal is not accomplished until out of His myriad creatures emerges a consciousness that can become Him — His double. Once He has duplicated Himself, He knows Himself, for He has succeeded in evolving a consciousness that is as great as He Himself. And so He closes down His shop, absorbing into Himself all His manifest creation, and returns into the void.

Until now we have been trying to second-guess the thoughts of the Creator in planning and organizing the universe *in His subjective space-time.* We have to emphasize that the events described until now did not yet take place in objective space-time; in other words, they were only His thoughts and were not yet manifest. You may remember from Chapter 4 that the highest level of consciousness occurs when the ‡ angle equals 90 degrees, that is, when the subjective time overlaps the objective space. This means that the subjective time is infinitely long, and a consciousness in that state fills all space, or is omnipresent. From Chapter 9 we know that in this state the consciousness is also omniscient. This is the angle or state at which the Creator *is* and thinks His universe.

As we said before, once He has decided to move, He begins by defining His boundaries — His real estate, so to speak. He does this by means of light; a sheath of light appears and outlines His body. This is not a light as we know it but of a level of energy peculiar to Him; it acts as a container for what we know as our manifest space-time. His body is very likely an ovoid that resembles an egg or a seed, and its size would be, naturally, the size of the universe.

All the above happenings are occurring in the subjective space and subjective time of the Creator since He is the being having the highest possible level of consciousness. His subjective time is therefore stretched out very much. In fact, He has an infinite amount of time to accomplish all that we are talking about. But to us simple mortals, who would be watching the action somehow from a distance, all this would occur suddenly because we spend most of our conscious time in objective time-space. Therefore, while the Creator can take His time to contemplate, design, and construct His universe at leisure, to us it would appear in a big bang. Suddenly the whole thing would just be there. And in order to find out objectively what is there, we have to start exploring His creation in our slowpoke way, bit by bit, and get ourselves entangled in the familiar space-time or time-like universe in which things happen in a more or less ordered sequence.

Let's return now and watch the Creator do His "thing" in His subjective space-time. We have watched Him outline His real estate, which was enveloped in a sheath of light. Within this shell his energy is at first diffuse. Next, His energy starts to polarize; there is a spatial separation of positive and negative energy (Fig. 51). This energy we shall call "protomatter," or the precursor of our matter. We now have positive and negative protomatter.

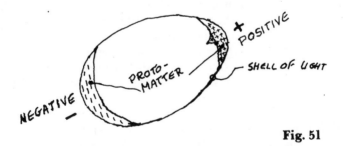

Fig. 51

Let us say that the positive energy has accumulated at the tip of the ovoid, the negative one at the bottom of it. A differential in energy or potential has thus arisen along the axes of the ovoid. In this way the relative aspect of the absolute is born. There is now a difference between the outside and the inside of the shell of light and a difference in energy between the two ends of the ovoid. A duality has arisen where there was none before.

The "AHA" moment

In the meantime, more and more energy is being built up at the poles of the ovoid. The ovoid is trembling from the great accumulation of potential energy, and then suddenly — zap! — a great spark flashes like a bolt of lightning across the void within the shell of light. A great thunderclap follows — the first "sound" — and the first act of fertilization has taken place (Fig. 52A). The impact of this discharge sets in motion the reservoir of negative protomatter, which rises in a great column as it is drawn to the opposite pole (Fig. 52B). It spreads out at the tip of the ovoid shell and runs down hugging its walls, back to the bottom of the shell (Fig. 52C). It continues to flow in the central column up to about half the height of the ovoid. Here, its energy exhausted, the column drops back into the negative energy pool at the bottom of the ovoid except for one drop of matter that separates from the column and remains floating — balanced between the two poles (Fig. 52D).* The flow of protomatter has prepared — or we may say "seeded" — the protospace for the

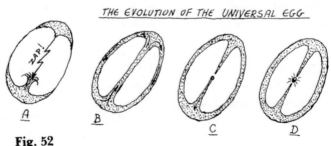

THE EVOLUTION OF THE UNIVERSAL EGG

Fig. 52

* The separation of droplets from a jet of fluid is a very common occurrence in fluid dynamics. When a high-voltage discharge occurs under the conditions shown in Figure 52A, and the fluid in the container happens to be a dielectric, the kind of behavior shown in Figures B, C, and D is very likely to occur.

appearance of the kind of physical matter we know. The flow of protomatter has outlined the volume to which our time-space will be confined. The sound of the great thunderclap is still reverberating within the shell.

This is the "Aha!" moment of the Creator. He has contemplated and thought for a long time, and now, finally and suddenly, He has seen the whole design in all its complicated detail, and in one great flash of creative insight He made the *potential* forms of the whole creation appear. This great sound, which contains all the possible frequencies, continuously reverberates within the shell, creating an infinite number of interference patterns of *potential* beings and event matrices. It outlines all that the Creator has visualized Himself to be. And so, having prepared the form, the space-time bound, visible, physical and nonphysical relative universe will appear. Matter will gradually fill the forms or molds created by the interference patterns in protospace. These forms and event patterns have been *visualized and seen* by the Creator in their entirety, from the beginning of time to the end of time, that is, starting from the white hole and ending in the black hole.

His focus has now become the droplet floating in the middle of the shell. The action of this droplet (the black and white hole) reflects the previous flow of protomatter through it. It becomes a focus, a source producing a flow of physical matter in the form of radiation to fill the event matrices — the interference patterns prepared by the reverberating sound.

This is the nucleus or the egg. It represents all the information about the universe in a condensed form, just as a seed represents a tree. The rest of the ovoid structure mirrors the same information in a manifest, "unfurled" form; that is, the actual tree. Again we apparently have two opposites, the seed and the tree, both containing the same information but in different form. One is potential form, reflecting the absolute, and one is a manifest, "unfurled" form, representing the relative realities, or the absolute in action.

We now know that the purpose of evolution is to produce consciousnesses of higher and higher order. The universe is a teaching and learning machine. Its purpose is to know itself. Knowledge is freely available in the universe like every other natural resource. It is there for everyone who is willing to make the effort to take it. We can poke around in our sequential "objective" time-space, or we can take the intuitive, subjective "time-space" route. Both are needed to get us there.

As creatures in all galaxies are going through their event patterns in this enormous hologram called the universe, we should remember that each element of volume in the hologram contains *all* the information about the whole grand design. In other words, "knowledge is structured in consciousness."

This is again Nature's little hint: "Study the micro and you'll find the macro reflected in it." Or if we study ourselves thoroughly, we may just find the design of the universe reflected in us.

There is no need to repeat to the intuitive reader what has been pointed out before: that an egg and all seeds reflect this basic design of the universe. Energy flows through the center of the egg along its long axis, turns around, and flows back over itself, forming an outside field of energy.

But then again, this may mean that the universal egg is just the seed produced by a much vaster system in which the egg of our universe is just a tiny cell among many cells, and that vaster system, in turn, is only a cell of an even vaster system, and that even much vaster system is again just a speck in an even vaster system, and . . .

Summary

Our objective reality is composed of a void filled with pulsating fields. If we stop the pulsations of the fields, we get back the absolute.

The absolute is where opposing extremes become reconciled and are merged. This is the level at which the Creator functions.

The Creator draws up the plans for His universe. These are the laws of Nature, the rules of the game.

His goal is the evolution of consciousness. He uses opposing forces of good and evil to stimulate evolution.

Even matrices are fields within the universe that affect our endocrine glands in particular preprogrammed ways, so that the most susceptible portion of mankind will behave in certain expected patterns.

When a unit of consciousness has developed to a point at which it understands that it is part of the Creator, the Creator will set him aside and assign to him some jobs to do. Eventually, such a consciousness will develop into a co-creator.

The creation of a universe starts by the separation of a part of the void, which is outlined by a sheath of light to form an ovoid shell. Then polarization of protomatter occurs. A discharge passes through the two poles of the ovoid and sets the protomatter moving.

The black-white hole nucleus in the center is the source of all matter in the universe.

It is possible that this universe is just a tiny cell in a much larger structure.

EPILOGUE

Back to the subjective space-time of our Creator.

Having produced another creator ("in His image He created him" . . .), the Creator takes off for the equivalent of a cosmic corner drug store — to hang around and talk shop and relax with the boys. He introduces and shows off His new double, who is yet naive, not having experienced the worries of a Creator. After having rested for a while, and having picked up a few useful tips for His next universe, the Creator is off for another round. On the way, for just a fraction of a second, a thought crosses His mind: "Who knows, after this round I may just get a promotion. . . ."

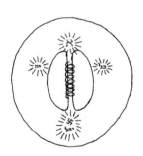

APPENDIX
STRESSES AND THE BODY

INTRODUCTION
STRESSES AND THE BODY

The joys and the woes of accelerated evolution

We tend to view the human nervous system just as any other organ in our body, as relatively static and unchanging. I would like to point out that our nervous system has a tremendous potential for development, and its development will occur through the normal biological evolution during the coming millennia. This evolution can be accelerated by utilizing certain techniques.

We said before that the human nervous system can be taught to function on different levels of consciousness or realities. Normally, this development is a lengthy process and can be achieved by systematic meditation, or it may occur spontaneously.

Over the years of my involvement with this area, I have seen many cases of spontaneous and systematic evolution of the nervous system. There are some physiological changes occurring in the body associated with the attainment of these different levels of evolution. These changes may come about slowly, over a period of years, and go unnoticed, or they may occur suddenly. Some of the symptoms resulting from these changes may be very mild and some very powerful, depending on the amount of stress accumulated in the body. "Stress accumulated in the body" may sound strange, but evidence is mounting to show that emotional stresses are imprinted on the physical body just as music is imprinted on a phonograph record. We know only very well that people, or even animals, may develop high blood pressure, and eventually heart attacks due to emotional stress. Others, with high levels of anxiety and frustration, may develop stomach ulcers or other ailments. A whole host of other physical symptoms may be attributed to psychological stress. In other words, psychosomatic diseases are an index of the amount of stress in the body.

Hans Selye, in his book *The Stress of Life,** describes these processes in depth. When a body is filled with stresses, the nervous system is so busy handling them that its potential for attaining higher states of consciousness is very limited. In other words, there is too much jitteriness or, in technical terms, too much "noise" in the system, which prevents the nervous system from rising to a higher level.

All schools of meditation, therefore, emphasize the importance of "calming down the body." But, of course, the stresses in the system are actually energy patterns, and they have to be converted and eliminated from the body. One of the most common forms into which these stresses are converted is body movement. It is not unusual to see people who are meditating go through different involuntary body movements, such as moving the arms, head, shaking of the whole body, etc. The heavier the stresses that are given off, the stronger the movements may become. There are other ways in which these stresses may come out. These are a direct release of emotions, which may take the form of depressions, crying, and general emotionalism. Other ways may manifest simply as temporary pain in different areas of the body.

All considered, meditation combined with light body-toning exercises, such as some hatha yoga postures and mild breathing exercises, can be the most effective, inexpensive, and fastest system for the removal of stresses from the body.

I don't want to give you the impression that anyone who meditates will have the symptoms described above. On the contrary, by far the largest majority of people who practice meditation have very pleasurable or even blissful sensations, and those who have any of the stress symptoms will eventually outgrow them as the level of stress in their bodies diminishes. They then begin to enjoy a feeling of growing inner peace and tranquillity, which is not obtainable by any other means.

* New York: McGraw-Hill, 1956 (paperback).

The Physio-Kundalini
Syndrome

Until now, we have dealt with just the garden variety of stress release. In this chapter, I would like to acquaint the reader with a specific problem that again is connected with the accelerated evolution of the nervous system. As has been mentioned before, the human nervous system has a tremendous latent capacity for evolution. This evolution can be accelerated either by meditative techniques, or it may occur spontaneously in an unsuspecting individual. In both cases, a sequence of events is triggered, causing sometimes strong and unusual bodily reactions and unusual psychological states. Some of those people who meditate may suspect that these reactions are somehow connected with meditation. Others, however, who develop these symptoms spontaneously, may panic and seek medical advice. (Sometimes individuals of both groups may seek medical advice.) Unfortunately, however, Western medicine is presently not equipped to handle these problems. Strangely, in spite of the intensity of the symptoms, little or no physical pathology can be found.

Most of the mild cases are dismissed as psychosomatic symptoms, while in severe cases either drastic radiological tests are undertaken or possibly exploratory surgery attempted.

The sequence of bodily symptoms usually starts at the left foot or toes, either as a mild tingling stimulus or as cramps. The stimulus continues up the left leg to the hip. In extreme cases, there is a paralysis of the foot and of the whole leg. Loss of sensation in large areas of the skin of the leg may occur. From the hip the stimulus moves up the spine to the head. Here sometimes severe headaches (pressurelike) may develop. In case of prolonged and severe pressures in the head, degeneration of the optical nerve may set in, with accompanying visual impairment. Loss of memory and general disorientation may occur.

The psychological symptoms tend to mimic schizophrenia. It is very likely, therefore, that such individuals may be diagnosed as schizophrenics and be either institutionalized or given very drastic and unwarranted treatment. It is ironic that persons in whom the evolutionary processes of Nature have begun to operate more rapidly, and who can be considered as advanced mutants of the human race, are institutionalized as subnormal by their "normal" peers. I dare to guess, on the basis of discussions with my psychiatrist-friends, that this process is not as exotic and rare as one would like to believe, and possibly 25 to 30 percent of all institutionalized schizophrenics belong to this category — a tremendous waste of human potential. It is my hope that as the material presented here gradually reaches the more open-minded physicians and psychotherapists, and as the syndrome described becomes more widely known, nontraumatic methods of dealing with these symptoms will be developed, methods that will not stop but slow down and control the rate at which the evolutionary process is progressing, thus allowing the "patients" to develop at a safe, acceptable rate and to function normally in everyday environment.

What is this mysterious "Kundalini"?

All the preceding descriptions make meditation, or just plain living, appear to be a very dangerous affair. Anyone can be hit out of the blue by mysterious symptoms, which Western medicine does not know how to handle. Let me assure you that just a very small percentage of people is so affected, and this also has its compensations. These symptoms are, after all, the correlates of spiritual development. It would, therefore, be wise for us to look into the literature dealing with such matters and see whether we can find descriptions of similar things happening in other cultures at other times.

The *kundalini*, as described in yoga literature, is said to be an "energy coiled up, like a serpent, at the base of the spine." When this energy is "awakened," it enters the spine, rises up along it, and is seen or perceived as a luminous serpent by the person having the experience. Once it has risen into the head, the luminous rod hopefully pierces the top of the head; that is, the rodlike energy beam is seen as projecting through the skull, pointing upward. When this happens, the person is said to be "illuminated." Eventually, such a person may become highly intuitive and develop some psychic powers, such as clairvoyance, clairaudience, or healing abilities. Whether he develops these or not depends on many factors. However, sometimes illumination may be late in coming, and all the person may be able to show for his efforts is a king-size headache, which may last for years.

The books on yoga also show several points in the body, seven in number. These are the so-called *chakras*, or energy centers. These centers are to be "vivified" or energized by the rising kundalini energy. When this happens, the centers become receptors and distributors of inflowing cosmic energy for the body. These *chakras* are located near major nerve plexuses and coincide more or less with the glands of our endocrine system. When these centers are energized, they affect the endocrine glands and through them our behavior and physical functioning. All this makes absolutely no sense from the point of view of Western physiology or medicine. However, the trouble with the just-described kundalini is that it works, whether we like it or not. And the symptoms our Western people are having correspond with the symptoms induced by the exotic, unbelievable kundalini.

In a way, this is similar to the acupuncture situation. The exotic acupuncture has proved itself in this country; it works, although Western science is still at a loss to describe *how* it works. The fault, naturally, does not lie with acupuncture but with our models of reality. That is, we are unable to look at this system in a way that would make sense to us because our angle of view is too narrow. Therefore, what we urgently need are models that would allow us to view these "queer" workings of the kundalini (and acupuncture) in terms that would make sense to us. This is what I shall attempt to do in the pages that follow.

Progressive sensory-motor cortex syndrome

This long title is used to describe the syndrome that seems to correspond well to the observed experiences of persons who have undergone the previously described sequence of symptoms, thus putting the esoteric kundalini into terms of Western physiology.

Having a background in biomedical engineering, I have tried to measure the changes induced by altered states of consciousness on the physiological states of the body.

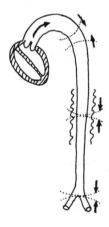

The results of some of these measurements have been given in Chapters 1 and 2, in which it is shown how the heart-aorta system goes into resonance, and how it entrains the body to move in a rhythmic, harmonic motion. A rather technical description of the physiological model, developed by me to explain the kundalini mechanism, appears in a book by Lee Sannella, M.D., titled: *Kundalini — Psychosis or Transcendence.* *

* Henry S. Dakin, Publ., 3101 Washington St., San Francisco, Cal. 94115, 1976.

Here again, I have to repeat my admonition: A model is only a model and describes only the mechanical-physiological portion of the kundalini "syndrome." The kundalini is a much larger concept in which planetary and spiritual forces come into play. However, even this limited model, as shown in my paper, is already a useful tool because it puts at the disposal of the medical profession a reasonable, working concept of a syndrome that until now has not been described at all.

The model describes the *sequence of symptoms* that allows the interviewing physician to compare the symptoms described by the patient. If the past pattern of symptoms fits the model, then the future symptoms are fairly predictable. The paper in Sannella's book is just a preliminary progress report. Much more work needs to be done to confirm some of the assumptions made in the paper.

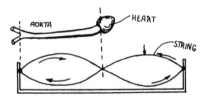

Kundalini: the ultimate stress-release mechanism

This model, which we may call the "physio-kundalini" since it deals only with the physiological part of the kundalini, describes the kundalini as a stimulus spreading along the sensory cortex of the two hemispheres, starting from the bottom of the cleft between the two hemispheres of the brain. The layout of points on the sensory or motor cortices corresponds to points in the body, so that when a point on the cortex, representing, for example, the knee, is electrically or mechanically stimulated, the person feels the stimulus in his knee. He has no way of knowing that the stimulus is caused by his brain being artificially stimulated.

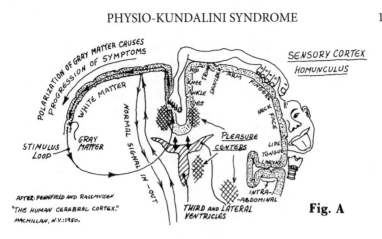

Fig. A

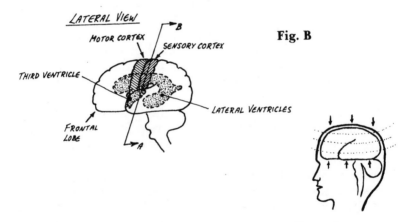

Fig. B

This sequence of points on the cortex is called the "homunculus" or the "little man," for if one draws a picture of the parts of the body to which the points in the cortex are connected, a distorted human form results (Fig. A). Both the sensory and motor cortices have approximately the same layout of these points.

I am trying to show that the layout of points on both the sensory and the motor cortices corresponds closely to the path the kundalini takes in the body. This path is described in esoteric literature (see Appendix Bibliography 1-4). Three actual recent case histories are given at the end of this chapter.

To cause such a stimulus to move along the cortex, accoustical standing waves in the cerebral ventricles are postulated. These standing waves are triggered by the heart sounds, and they cause vibrations in the walls of the ventricles. The ventricles are fluid-filled cavities in the brain. Figure B shows the position of the third and lateral ventricles (stippled areas), and the strips of tissue (hatched), that make up the sensory and motor cortices of the brain. Figure A represents a cross-section of the brain along line A-B of Figure B. The vibrations that arise in the ventricles are conducted to the gray matter of the cortex which lines the fissure between the two hemispheres (Fig. A). These vibrations will stimulate and eventually "polarize" the cortex in such a way that it will tend to conduct a signal along the homunculus, starting from the toes and up. This is shown in Figure A by a line of arrows forming a closed loop. This behavior is in contrast to the way the brain normally handles a signal, which is shown by the two lines, one ascending to the cortex and one descending from it. The normal signal leads into the cortex at right angles to it.

The states of bliss described by those whose kundalini symptoms have completed the full loop along the hemispheres may be explained as a self-stimulation of the pleasure centers in the brain, caused by the circulation of a "current" along the sensory cortex. Figure A shows pleasure centers located in the path of the "current" loop in both hemispheres, just below the toes of the homunculus. When body motion develops due to the action of the circulating stimulus "current" we have to assume that there is "crosstalk" between the sensory cortex and the neighboring motor cortex (Fig. B).

That most of the described symptoms start on the left side of the body means that it is mostly a development occurring in the right hemisphere. This stands to reason because we are using our reasoning, rational, logical, linearly-thinking left hemisphere all the time, while meditation tends to stimulate the nonverbal, feeling, intuitive right hemisphere.

My model also suggests that the spontaneous cases of kundalini may be attributed, among other things, to periodic exposure to certain mechanical or acoustical vibrations in our normal environment, which will cause the sequence of symptoms to arise. This has been shown by a biofeedback technique utilizing a pulsating magnetic field around the head. When people are exposed to frequencies of about 4 or 7 Hz. for prolonged periods of time, as may happen simply by repeatedly riding in a car whose suspension and seat combination produce that range of vibration, or being exposed for long periods of time to these frequencies caused, for instance, by an air-conditioning duct. The cumulative effect of these vibrations may be able to trigger a spontaneous physio-kundalini sequence in susceptible people who have a particularly sensitive nervous system.

I would like to emphasize that when a person is healthy, relaxed, and generally free from psychological stress, these symptoms go unnoticed. Only when the unfolding kundalini reaches *areas of stress in the body* do the symptoms become troublesome. The symptoms will persist until the stresses in that particular area of the body are released. This will then usually appear as localized pain. When that happens, the kundalini moves on until it reaches the next spot of stress in its path. The severity of symptoms is always proportional to the degree of stress encountered. When the kundalini has run its course, the body is basically free of deep-seated stresses, and since the body is reflected in the cortex, we may say that the brain is also relieved of stresses. Thus, the kundalini is a great stress-relieving system. It will not allow the further accumulation of stress in the body. Once the full circuit is operating smoothly, stresses will be eliminated from the system as rapidly as they build up, so that no permanent accumulation of stress is possible.

It is interesting to note that in some types of epilepsy there is also a sequence of symptoms, sometimes called the "march of epilepsy." Here the sequence runs in the opposite direction from that of kundalini. In an epeleptic, the lip area may be affected first, then the face; eventually, the symptoms spread down the neck, through the shoulders, into the arms, and eventually to the legs. The kundalini would seem, therefore, to be a natural antidote to certain types of epilepsy. Meditation would thus be a reasonable treatment for this disease.

The "coming of age" of the nervous system

When the kundalini has finally completed its circuit, it can be said that the human nervous system has achieved what is analogous to the state of puberty in the body in the sense that it can start functioning more fully on ever higher levels of consciousness. That is, the nervous system has achieved a "young adult" status, and can assume a more responsible role.

After a while, one may find some peculiar stimulation around the solar plexus or navel areas, which may occur mostly at night, when lying on one's back, and the feeling will be that of energy flowing into the body through those areas. One may feel some internal organs being stimulated by these energies. What is happening now is that the nervous system has become sufficiently refined, so that it may enter into resonance with outside energies. These may be energies associated with the activities of the planet and the sun. Many of the electromagnetic oscillations within the planetary field occur at physiological frequencies.

I hope that you still remember what was said in Chapter 9 about the rudimentary consciousness of the planet and the higher consciousness, which uses the planet as a place to hang its hat on, so to speak. Once a person's nervous system has developed to this point, energies provided by these high consciousnesses begin to flow automatically into the nervous system of the recipient due to a state of resonance with the above beings. This will cause further evolution of the nervous system, and eventually these consciousnesses may make themselves known in ways that are individually matched to each person's needs and abilities. Later, an unfolding of knowledge occurs that opens up broader and broader vistas about the workings of Nature, so that a person starts feeling that he is very much a part, and indeed a very active part, of Nature and the universe. When this happens, there is naturally a lot of excitement about these developments. It is best then for such a person to keep a calm, balanced attitude about all the goings on and not to be over-distracted by these occurrences. A steady routine in daily life is important. This will tend to counterbalance the more exciting events that may occur in or out of meditation.

All that was described above may happen to people *spontaneously*, that is, to people who do not meditate. However, it is usually associated then with much more trauma and results very frequently in the hospitalization of such people. The usual diagnosis will be schizophrenia. The reason for this is that they have been catapulted suddenly into a situation in which they are functioning in *more than one reality*. They can see and hear things occurring in our neighboring realities, that is the astral or other higher realities, because their "frequency response" has been broadened. However, since they did not have a gradual systematic evolution that meditation affords, they cannot handle the situation. The onslaught of information may be overwhelming, and they begin to mix and confuse two or three realities.

This confusion eventually surfaces, and the person so afflicted will seek help by trying to share his experiences with friends or relatives. He will be advised to seek medical help. The treatment, depending on the symptoms, could involve heavy sedatives, electroshock, or both, which may irrevocably damage a highly sensitive nervous system. Naturally, this becomes a regrettable situation.

In such *spontaneous cases* of development, in which severe bodily symptoms, such as strong headaches, pressures in the eyes, or other symptoms are present over a long period of time, permanent impairment of mental or physical function may occur.

However, *people who meditate* have milder symptoms, and they are unlikely to discontinue meditation because of occasional problems. Having reached a certain level of development of their nervous system through continuous practice, they realize that these are temporary obstacles on the way, until a total purification of the nervous system from stress is achieved.

It is clear that to handle the problems we have just discussed, the available medical treatments cannot be very helpful. Normal medical treatments cannot alleviate these problems, and if they do, it will occur only at a great cost to the patient in terms of his spiritual evolution. I hope that in the future medical centers capable of properly dealing with these problems will arise. The beginnings are already visible. Presently still in the conceptual stage, the so-called "holistic medical centers"* will be staffed by physicians and psychotherapists who have themselves experienced the symptoms described above or have been trained to understand them and thus will know how to handle their patients with sufficient care so as not to destroy their achievement as far as the fine tuning of their nervous system is concerned. As more and more physicans take up meditation, it is inevitable that a good percentage of them will be drawn to do just this kind of work. Natural psychic healers, who understand these processes, should have a place in such holistic medical centers, just as should the chiropractors, osteopaths, acupuncturists, etc., people who understand the flow of energies through the body.

Such holistic medical centers will be able to deal not only with the medical aspects of a health situation but also with its spiritual component.

The psychological aspects of the accelerated development of the nervous system are very well described by Roberto Assagioli, an Italian psychiatrist and founder of the "Psychosynthesis" movement in psychiatry. This movement is a part of the trend within psychiatry and psychotherapy to recognize the essential spirituality of man and to develop new methods of dealing with problems arising due to an accelerated development of the nervous system and its accompanying spiritual correlates.

The following is a quotation from Assagioli's book *Psychosynthesis:*

> In the following analysis of the vicissitudes and incidents which occur during the process of spiritual development, we shall consider both the successive stages of self-actualization and the achievement of full self-realization.
>
> Man's spiritual development is a long and arduous journey, an adventure through strange lands full of surprises, difficulties and even dangers. It involves a drastic transmutation of the "normal" elements of the personality, an awakening of potentialities hitherto dormant, a raising of

* Holistic means treating the whole man.

consciousness to new realms, and a functioning along a new inner dimension.

We should not be surprised, therefore, to find that so great a change, so fundamental a transformation, is marked by several critical states, which are not infrequently accompanied by various nervous, emotional and mental troubles. These may present to the objective clinical observation of the therapist *the same symptoms as those due to more usual causes,* but they have in reality quite another significance and function, and need very different treatment.

The incidence of disturbances having a spiritual origin is rapidly increasing nowadays, in step with the growing number of people who, consciously or unconsciously, are groping their way towards a fuller life. Moreover, the heightened development and complexity of the personality of modern man and his more critical mind have rendered spiritual development a more difficult and complicated process.

It is a combination of psychological and physical therapy that will alleviate the problems we have discussed above.

Table 1 shows 10 documented cases of the physio-kundalini syndrome. The sequence of symptoms is shown in Figure C. As the stimulus moves up the spine to a point facing each frontal *chakra,* it will be referred forward to stimulate the *chakras* that correspond to major nerve plexuses located in the pelvis, the solar plexus, the heart, the throat, and the head. It appears that the purpose of this syndrome is to unite the cerebro-spinal and the autonomic nervous systems, thus providing for a possible control of autonomic functions like respiration, cardiac function, blood flow, etc., through the cerebrospinal system. This indeed has been shown in studies performed on yogis who could easily control body functions that in the West were thought impossible to control, for example, heart beat, superficial blood circulation, etc. (Ref. 8).

This is the next stage in the evolution of our nervous system, and it is a necessary correlate of spiritual development, toward which all mankind is moving.

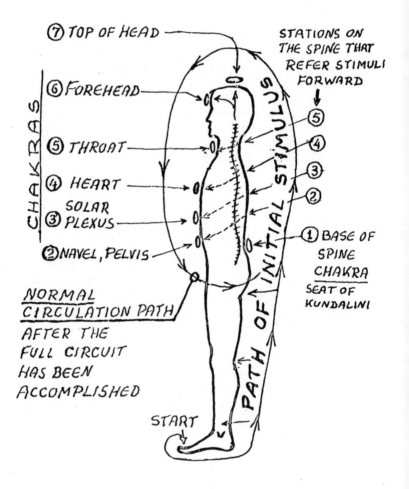

Fig. C

THREE REPORTED CASES OF KUNDALINI

Artist: F, 48 years old

She started Transcendental Meditation and after about five years began to experience occasional tinglings in her arms and heat in the hands. She did not sleep for days, with energy surging through her whole body, and had several "dreams" of having her consciousness separated from her body. A continuous loud sound had appeared inside her head. Soon there were cramps in her big toes, followed by vibratory feelings in her legs. Overnight, her big toe nails darkened as if hit by a hammer and eventually partially separated from the flesh. The tissues in her legs felt "torn through" by vibratory sensations. The vibrations spread to her lower back and swept over her body from lower back up to her head, forming a sensation of a band around the head, just above the eyebrows. Then her head started to move spontaneously. Later, her body moved sinuously, and her tongue pressed to the roof of her mouth. Then she sensed a strong sound of "om" there. The tinglings spread back of her neck and head, over the head to her forehead and face. Both nostrils were stimulated, causing a feeling of elongation of the nose. The tinglings then spread down her face. At times, her eyes seemed to move separately, and the pupils felt like holes that bored into her head and met in the center. Then she felt a tremendous head pressure and a brilliant light, followed by bliss and laughter. The tinglings spread farther down to her upper lip, chin, and mouth. About this time, there were dreams of heavenly music. Then the sensations went to her throat, chest, and abdomen, and eventually she felt as if there were a closing of the circuit in the shape of an egg, up through the spine, down through the front of the body. As it developed, the circuit activated particular *chakras* on its way, starting in the lower abdomen, then navel, the solar plexus, the heart, then the head centers. The last to be activated was the throat. After that, there was a continuous feeling of energy pouring into the body through the navel area. This feeling stopped after the "circuit" was completed. The whole experience had strong sexual overtones. The greater part of this activity occurred over several months. In the last two years, there has been only occasional activity, mostly during meditation or when she is relaxed in bed.

During the experiences, there was spontaneous yogic breathing (faint and controlled). Eventually, there developed head pressures, which centered around the back of the head, the top, and the forehead. They affected the eyes, and the vision had deteriorated. The pressures would become especially severe during reading, resulting in pressures in the eyes and a pulsing sensation at the top of the head.

The loud sound inside the head had eventually disappeared. Throughout the experience she understood that she was undergoing the rising of kundalini because she had read about it before. Therefore, she felt relaxed about it and just allowed things to happen. However, the situation developed into an emotional disorientation and a difficulty in integrating these experiences with the daily activities.

Since the inflow of energy prevented normal sleep for months and continued during the day as well, work became inefficient, and she felt as if she were completely detached and was witnessing her own activities. Eventually, she brought the situation under control. The general effect was a greater emotional stability and elimination of tension, along with a greatly enhanced intuitive insight.

Scientist: M, 53 years old

He started TM meditation and within five years began to have gross, thrashing body movements during meditation and at night in bed. After a few weeks, these subsided.

Months later, on going to bed, he felt tingling in his lower legs, followed by cramping in his big toes. The cramping extended to other muscles and gradually faded. The tingling rose to his lower back, and he "saw" a reddish light there. The light became like a rod, which he felt and saw being pushed up his spine. Then it extended forward to the umbilical area, with many tingling, vibrating sensations. Step by step, it proceeded in the spine to the level of his heart and then extended forward to stimulate the cardiac plexus before continuing upward. When it reached his head, he "saw" floods of white light, as if his skull were lit up from inside. Then the light seemed to spout out the top of his head as a solid beam. Sometime later, he felt a vibration in his right wrist, arm, and also in his left leg. As soon as he attended to these sensations, they disappeared. Then came a feeling of currents running through his shoulders and arms as "waves of current," occurring at three to four per second, later increasing to seven and more per second. At one time, when he focused on the center of his head, violent, uncontrollable spasms and convulsions came on.

At various times during all of this activity, he was aware of sounds in his head, mostly of high-pitched whistling and hissing. At other times, he heard flutelike musical tones. Very frequently there were feelings of peace and bliss.

His sleep began to be disturbed by "automatic" movements of his body. Sometimes he would awaken to find himself doing spontaneous yogic breathing and assuming various hatha yoga positions. After several nights of this, the tingling went to his forehead, nostrils, cheeks, mouth, and chin. During this process he had many ecstatic feelings and sexual stimulation, when the activity centered in the pelvic area. Then all this ceased and returned from time to time when he relaxed at night in bed. He could shut these off by turning on his side.

About a year later, pressures developed in his head at night and started moving downward. Simultaneously, a tingling sensation started moving up from the stomach. He "saw" this all happening to him as if from a distance. The two stimuli met at his throat. He felt as if a hole appeared in his throat at the point at which they met. From this "hole" all manner of purely spontaneous sounds were emitted. He had little control over these, about six months later the stimulus moved down from his throat to the abdomen, where it remained for a few months. Then they moved farther down into the pelvis.

This scientist had an inherently sensitive nervous system, but his awareness that he was going through the rise of kundalini and his knowledge of what to expect, together with the stabilizing effect of a meditative discipline, made him less susceptible to the disorganizing aspects of Kundalini. He realized that the difficulties he did have were the result of overstrenuous meditative practice, so he developed no anxieties during the process.

Artist: F, 53 years old

For years she has practiced hatha yoga for exercise but has never engaged in any type of meditation. Thirteen years ago she developed lower back pain with foot drop and partial paralysis of the left leg, so that she was put in traction for several weeks. The paralysis lasted for several months, while the left toe was also anesthetized. She felt a sensation like ants crawling on the skin of her leg, with cramps and tingling on the outside and back of the leg to the back of the knee, thigh, and hip. These conditions lasted intermittently for long periods of time. Twice she experienced a blackening of her big toe nail, which lasted for some time. Her back pain was diagnosed as sciatica and osteoporosis. The function of the legs gradually returned over the years since.

In the last three to four years, she has experienced left hip pain, usually in the summer. (X-ray shows nothing abnormal.) For two years there has been left hand weakness and heaviness with a dull pain.

On occasion of having to give an important talk, she developed anxiety and severe pain between her shoulder blades. Then she could not talk or move and hardly could breathe. This subsided gradually and returned several times since. X-rays said to have shown spondylosis.

For many years, since childhood, she had cramps and tingling of legs, migraine with scintillating scotoma, nausea and left-sided headaches.

In the last year or more, she developed loss of color vision and visual impairment in the left eye. Her intraocular tension is normal. The diagnosis is progressive degeneration of the optic nerve due to a "mass" (unspecified) in back of the eye orbit. Her mother had glaucoma.

Cortisone has recently been advised for a thyroid disorder — also worse on the left side. She has some exophthalamos and optic atrophy. Recently, she took radioactive iodine for diagnostic purposes, and 24 hours later saw almost clearly for 20 minutes.

During her pregnancy, her sensitivity to sight, taste and smell was much enhanced.

In the interview with this person, it became clear that she has a highly developed nervous system. She was aware of the activity of her head *chakra* — "the top of my head was open all the time" — although she did not understand the meaning of it. She was aware of higher realities already as a child but did not think that there was anything unusual about it and assumed that everybody else saw the way she did — "they just don't talk about it." As a child, she was told by her parents: "Come down from the skies, come down to earth."

Being engaged in hatha yoga for many years has stimulated and accelerated the activity of the *chakras* and is probably responsible for the rise of kundalini. The results of a spontaneous kundalini are clearly shown by her medical record. The symptoms started from the left toe, rising up the leg to the pelvis, the ensuing paralysis of the left leg, further rising up the spine into the neck (thyroid) and the head. The pressures in the head, developed due to kundalini, caused a degeneration of the optic nerve.

TABLE 1. PHYSIO-KUNDALINI SYMPTOMS

	SUBJECT			PHYSICAL SYMPTOMS ORDER OF OCCURRENCE						
No.	Age	Sex	Years meditates	Toes	Foot	Leg	Pelvis	Spine	Neck	Head
1	53	F	no	+	+	+++	+++	++	+	+++
2	48	F	yes 9	++	+	++	+	+	+	+++
3	29	F	yes 4			+	+	+	+	+++
4	52	M	yes 9	+	+	+	+	+	+	+
5	41	F	yes 8		+		+	+	+	+
6	50	M	yes 9			+	+	+	+	+
7	27	M	yes 2					+	+	+
8	37	M	yes 4		+	+	+	+	+	+
9	28	F	yes 3	+	+++	+++	+++	+		
10	29	F	yes 1	+	+++	+++	+++	+		

REMARKS
1: Spontaneous development, severe symptoms, paralysis of leg, visual impairment.
9: Paralysis of leg, foot drop.
10: Paralysis of leg, foot drop.

Degree of severity
of symptoms

Mild	Medium	Severe
+	++	+++

PSYCHOLOGICAL SYMPTOMS

Eye	Face	Throat	Abdomen	Headaches	Depression	Hallucinations	Unusual sensations	Visual aberration	Anxiety	Blissful states
++	+++			+++	+++				++	
+++	+	+	+	+++	+++		+	+	+	+
+	++	+	+	+++	+++		+		+++	
	+	+	+				+			++
	+			++	+	+	++		+++	++
+.	+									+
	+		+	+		+	+		+	
	+	+	+	+++			+		+	
					+		+		++	
					+++		+		+++	

Appendix
Bibliography

1. Leadbeater. *The Chakras.* Wheaton, Ill.: Theosophical Publishing House;
2. Krishna, Gopi. *Kundalini.* Berkeley, Calif.: Shambala Publications, 1970; London: The Watkins Publishing Co., 1970.
3. ——. *The Awakening of Kundalini.* New York: E. P. Dutton, 1975.
4. Rele, Vasant, G. *The Mysterious Kundalini.* Fort, Bombay: D. V. Taraporevala Sons & Co., Ltd.
5. Assagioli, Roberto. *Psychosynthesis.* New York: Viking Press, 1965; London: Turnstone Press, 1975.
6. Sannella, Lee, M.D. *Kundalini-Psychosis or Transcendence.* San Francisco: Henry S. Dakin, 1976.
7. *A Demonstration of Voluntary Control of Bleeding and Pain.* Research Department, The Meninger Foundation, Topeka, Kansas.
8. Rama, Swami. *Voluntary Control Project.* Research Department, Meninger Foundation, Topeka, Kansas.